*Winter Gra*

*also by Kathleen R. Fischer*
*published by Paulist Press*

THE INNER RAINBOW
THE FIRST TWO YEARS OF MARRIAGE (with Thomas N. Hart)

Kathleen R. Fischer

# *Winter Grace*

## Spirituality for the
## Later Years

*Paulist Press*    *New York/Mahwah*

The Publisher gratefully acknowledges the use of the following materials: Excerpt from "Shadows" from *The Complete Poems of D. H. Lawrence,* edited by Vivian de Sola Pinto and F. Warren Roberts, copyright © 1964 by Angelo Ravagli and C. M. Weekley, executors of the Estate of Frieda Lawrence Ravagli, is reprinted by permission of Viking Penguin, Inc. and Lawrence Pollinger Limited, London; excerpt from "The Love Song of J. Alfred Prufrock" from *Collected Poems 1909–1962* by T. S. Eliot copyright 1936 by Harcourt Brace Jovanovich, Inc., copyright © 1963 and 1964 by T. S. Eliot is reprinted by permission of Faber and Faber Publishers, London and Harcourt Brace Jovanovich, Inc.; excerpts from May Sarton, *Collected Poems 1930–1973,* New York: W. W. Norton, 1974 are used by permission of W.W. Norton & Company, Inc. and Russell & Volkening, Inc.; excerpt from "Isaac and Archibald" by Edwin Arlington Robinson from *Selected Poems of Edwin Arlington Robinson,* copyright 1915 by Edwin Arlington Robinson, renewed 1943 by Ruth Nivison, is reprinted by permission of Macmillan Publishing Company; "With Age Wisdom" from *The Human Season* by Archibald MacLeish, copyright © 1972 by Archibald MacLeish, is reprinted by permission of Houghton Mifflin Company. Biblical quotations are from *The Jerusalem Bible,* copyright 1966 by Darton, Longman & Todd Ltd., and Doubleday & Company, Inc.

Library of Congress
Catalog Card Number: 84-61975

ISBN: 0-8091-2675-3

Published by Paulist Press
997 Macarthur Boulevard
Mahwah, New Jersey 07430

Printed and bound in the
United States of America

# CONTENTS

# INTRODUCTION

By the year 2000 there will be over thirty-five million persons in the United States sixty-five or older. Estimates are that by the year 2050 that number will double. This phenomenon of a large aging population is clearly one of the most significant developments of our century. It affects each of us. We all have older parents, relatives, and friends. We are all aging ourselves.

Thanks to research in the field of aging, we now better understand many of the physical, psychological, social, and economic aspects of the aging process. But we have not yet fully answered the deeper questions emerging from our longer life expectancy. Is this lengthening of human life an anomalous triumph of science and technology over purpose and meaning? Does anyone know how to live the last years meaningfully and joyfully?

It is precisely here that the need for a spiritual perspective is most acutely felt. Since the spiritual is interwoven with all other aspects of life, we cannot fully treat human aging without attention to this dimension, especially where meaning is concerned. In fact, we cannot really understand *any* stage of our life journey unless we can penetrate the mystery of its final stage.

As a theologian and counselor, I am frequently asked hard questions about religious dimensions of the later years. This book brings together my reflections on that topic, reflections which have been sharpened in dialogue with others through teaching and counseling. I explore the Christian perspective on several key experiences of these years: memories, dependence and independence, love and sexuality, loss, dying, and resurrection. The book is intended for older persons themselves and for their friends and families. It is designed as a resource for those who work with older adults, as well as for anyone who wants to find the spiritual opportunities in his or her own aging process. The premise of the book is that Christian faith can transform the last decades of life.

Interacting with older adults has blessed and changed my life immeasurably. It is older people who have shown me the pain and difficulties of the later years. And it is they who have revealed to me the riches and positive possibilities of these years. Finally, they have opened my eyes to the great diversity which exists among them, a diversity which shatters the usual stereotypes. I draw extensively on the lives of people whom I have known as friends and relatives, as well as those with whom I have worked in community settings and nursing homes. I have changed their names and the details of their lives in order to respect their privacy, but I am immensely grateful for all they have contributed to this book.

The later years take us into the heart of the central Christian paradox of death/resurrection. It is in living the pattern of that mystery that people discover the graces of life's winter season and share them with us all.

# 1

# SPIRITUALITY AND AGING

A great deal of ambiguity permeates our thinking about aging. Is it a decline or an ascent? Should we describe life as a journey that moves upward until it peaks about middle age and then slopes downward to death? Shall we work to prevent aging or learn to revere it? The physical sciences have pointed to the irreversible, physiological deterioration that accompanies aging. The social sciences add information about social isolation, loss of income, and increased dependence on others. In order to counteract these negative interpretations of aging, recent writers have tried to show that the later years can, in fact, be the best years of our lives. Given good health and economic security we can remain active, independent, and socially and professionally involved. Some even talk about "growing young" as a way of emphasizing the positive values of aging. In an effort to demonstrate that aging need not be equated with disease and loss, such positive approaches have sometimes bypassed the real losses that accompany aging.

We cannot learn to understand aging if we undervalue or overvalue its realities, or if we simply try to make it appear as much like midlife or youth as possible. As the anthropologist Barbara Myerhoff says of the Jewish elderly portrayed in her book *Number Our Days,* externally they are cut off, poor, and immobile.[1] They are, in fact, these things. But they are also engaged, resourceful, vigorous, and independent. Psychologist Robert Coles witnessed the same thing in the old people he interviewed in New Mexico. Now in their seventies and eighties, they have long memories of the hardships they have faced and only partially surmounted. Yet they are men and women deeply convinced that they are eminently valuable human beings, worthy of the love, admiration, and respect of their children and grandchildren.[2]

The fact is that aging is *both* descent and ascent, *both* loss and gain. This is true of growth at every stage of the life cycle: childhood, adolescence, midlife, and old age. Time is both life and death. Change encompasses both emerging and perishing. At every point in the human journey we find that we have to let go in order to move forward; and letting go means dying a little. In the process we are being created anew, awakened afresh to the source of our being. Aging is a paradox, the unity of apparent contradictions. Jesus challenges his followers with this paradox when he says, "For anyone who wants to save his life will lose it; but anyone who loses his life for my sake will find it" (Mt 16:25). Emptiness can somehow be fullness, weakness can be strength, and dying can lead to new life. A spirituality of aging must help us find a way to turn losses into gains, to learn how the stripping process which often accompanies aging can be a gradual entrance into freedom and new life, how, in fact, aging can be winter grace.

Winter is a season of some very real losses. The flowers of springtime are gone; leaves fall. Trees stand bare and revealed. But from these losses there are gifts to be had. As May Sarton says in her poem, "The Contemplation of Wisdom":

> Partaking wisdom, I have been given
> The sum of many difficult acts of grace,
> A vital fervor disciplined to patience.
> This cup holds grief and balm in equal measure,
> Light, darkness. Who drinks from it must change.
>     . . . .
> Yet I am lavish with riches made from loss.[3]

Winter reveals those things that summer conceals. We can see farther and with clearer vision. Paths that were clogged with vines or leaves in summer and fall open up, and we can walk in places not possible in other seasons. There is an inner life and awakening; beneath the shell of the bud is sap in gestation, and the colors of spring tinge the nudity of winter. Annie Dillard describes it aptly in *Pilgrim at Tinker Creek:* "I bloom indoors in the winter like a forced forsythia; I come in to come out."[4]

What are the graces of winter? The word "grace" has many meanings. So, too, the graces of the later years take many forms. We describe beauty of movement as grace. The rhythm of old age may be slower than that of youth, but it can reveal a new kind of beauty, one refined by experience. Graciousness and mercy are other aspects of grace. Old age can be a time of larger love and compassion, of attitudes of good will and thoughtfulness toward others. We call a temporary exemption or reprieve a grace period. Since we all stand under the certain sentence of death, the gift of several additional years of life is such a period of grace. We also speak of being graced by another's presence; the graces of winter reach into all our lives as we and our society are changed by contact with the old. On another level, grace is the entry of God into human life, the unmerited love and favor God shows us. The graces of winter are not simply a matter of trying harder; they are divine gifts, and these gifts are always somehow transforming. They appear in the shape of the grace of Christ, as gifts of life emerging from a struggle with the forces of death.

We understand the meaning of winter grace best when we see it embodied in the lives of older individuals. On August 6, 1976, Dorothy Day, foundress of the Catholic Worker Movement, made her last speaking appearance before a large audience. It was the afternoon session of the Eucharistic Congress at Philadelphia. Dorothy was now seventy-nine, and those attending the Congress recall that her appearance was one of extreme frailty. She was dressed, as usual, in clothing that had probably come from the bins of the Catholic Worker houses. Yet her fragile appearance strengthened rather than weakened the impact of her brief remarks. She spoke of convictions that had fired her life for half a century: her love of God, and our vocation to bring that love to all of creation; her attraction to the physical aspects of the Church—bread, wine, water, the sound of waves and wind; our need for repentance and forgiveness; the unity of all humanity. She was only a few years away from her own death in November 1980; yet Dorothy Day was a source of grace and power for those who heard her. Such gifts of love emerging from weakness are winter grace.

The paradox that Dorothy Day embodied in her last years was also captured by the Spanish artist Goya. He once drew a picture of an old man, showing all the signs of his advancing years. Next to the picture is the caption: "I'm still learning." The old man was Goya himself. Though deaf, Goya continued to grow in freshness and originality, recording the atrocities of war on canvases that evoke indignant compassion in viewers. In the second half of his life, in spite of pain and sickness, he moved from restraint to freedom, from timidity to boldness. This sense of human possibility in the midst of limitations is winter grace.

Winter grace is also the capacity to affirm life in the face of death. Several years ago my father-in-law, a man in his seventies, was dying of cancer. In and out of his room moved several of his nine children, wanting to be with him at the end or to provide some comfort during his last hours. His breathing was slow and labored; his consciousness came and went like flickering shafts of sunlight against a darkening sky. The first grandson to carry his name to the next generation had been born a few days earlier and brought to his bedside. And on the last day of his life, in the midst of restless hours of sleep and waking, he struggled to sit up, painfully held out his arms, and very slowly said, with a warm smile on his face, "Let's go see that baby again."

Winter grace appears in other forms. In Ingmar Bergman's motion picture *Wild Strawberries,* a seventy-six year old Swedish doctor, Isak Borg, receives the highest honor in his field, a Jubilee Doctorate which marks fifty years of service. Yet he also faces a creative despair hidden in his inner self. Borg has outlived nine brothers and sisters, and has been a widower for many years. He had been a good doctor, but finds himself alone in old age. As he drives with his daughter-in-law Marianne to the ceremony in the city of Lund, Borg faces the lack of affection and withholding of self that have characterized his life. He shares with Marianne his growing realization that he is dead, although he is alive. This admission becomes the turning point. Borg begins to let love re-enter his life, reaching out in friendship, forgiveness, and care to his housekeeper, his daughter-in-law, and his son. By the end of the day his ceremonial honor is transcended by the depth of insight he has gained and by the new unity he experiences with his family.

Winter grace also takes shape in the ninety-eight year old Buddhist monk Nichidatsu Fujii. Age has weakened his body; his feet hurt and his legs must be rubbed intermittently to restore circulation. Yet he continues to address peace gatherings, speaking out with clarity and conviction about the evils of nuclear weaponry. The contours of winter grace are there in the eighty year old woman who returns to school to pursue the degree in literature she has always wanted, and in the recently widowed woman in her sixties who moves out of her own loss to help a pair of struggling newlyweds. It appears in the man of ninety-four who has a pacemaker and three chronic diseases, but spends his time in laughter and outreach to others. Returning from a grade school where he has spent the afternoon telling stories in history classes, he says with delight: "Not one of them took any notes; yet they could repeat for me almost word for word the stories I told." Winter grace is courage grown larger in the face of diminishment.

### The Meaning of Spirituality and Aging

One reason for the ambiguity surrounding aging is the fact that we have viewed it from an exclusively biological perspective. Although studies of aging have expanded dramatically during the last two decades, few have taken a spiritual view. Consequently, individuals often fear aging as a downhill battle, a gradual decrease in vitality and increase in vulnerability. The growing edge of discussion on the meaning of aging is its spiritual dimension.

But the term spiritual can itself be misleading. One understanding of the spiritual is that which is immaterial, in contrast to bodily or material. When life is divided up into compartments, physical, social and emotional needs are seen as existing alongside another area called spiritual. This spiritual life is usually equated with church-going, prayers, and religious devotions. In other words, it becomes a separate set of activities, a separate area of life. This is not the understanding of spiritual intended here.

By spirituality is meant, not one compartment of life, but the deepest dimension of all of life. The spiritual is the ultimate ground of all our questions, hopes, fears, and loves: our efforts to deal creatively with retirement and to find a purpose for our lives after our family has been raised; our struggles with the loss of a spouse or the move from a home of many years; questions of self-worth and fear of reaching out to make new friendships; the discovery of new talents, deeper peace, wider boundaries of love. All these are spiritual concerns. Christian spirituality involves the entire human person in all of his or her relationships. Some recent studies show, in fact, that while older persons feel more need for religious undergirding in their lives than ever before, they attend church services less.[5] There are many reasons for this, among them health and transportation problems. But church services can also seem far removed from the real life questions faced by older people. They want to know how faith illumines the realities experienced in the aging process itself. A spirituality of aging must begin then with our very existence as older persons.

Describing the experiences of the later years is difficult. For one thing, it is hard to define a fabric as variously textured as aging itself. Many older people tell me that they regard age as a mental concept; you are as old as you think you are, as old as you feel. What they are pointing to is the truth that how we age depends on the way we internalize society's images of the old. When we start to see ourselves as used up and useless, we begin to act accordingly. Not only does the manner in which people respond to change vary, but changes associated with aging do not occur all at once for an individual, and no two individuals experience exactly the same changes at the same stage of their lives.

We can be at different ages at one and the same time in terms of our mental, physical, and emotional capacities. Many physical, social, and economic variables affect the way individuals age. It has also become clear that the decades of one's fifties and sixties can be very different from the seventh, eighth and ninth decades of life. To make this point we have begun to speak of the "young old" and the "old old," with the age of seventy-five as a convenient dividing line. The "young old" are often a relatively healthy group, married and still living with their spouses in their own homes, and active in their neighborhoods and communities. They are generally vigorous and well educated, and very different from society's stereotypes of old age.

Another factor makes generalizations about the later years difficult. Though our stereotyping of the elderly has led us to view them as basically similar, there is probably no other point in life when personal diversity is so apparent. A lifetime of accumulated differences in experience, education, and social opportunities has sharpened individuality. As we grow older we become more ourselves, more unique. This applies as much to the spiritual dimension of our lives as to any other, although the religious may be the last realm of stereotyping of the elderly to die. Our spirituality in the later years is marked by the unique and varied faith journey each of us has taken.

Perhaps more influential than any of these factors is the way in which our society has distorted the experience of aging. Simone de Beauvoir established some time ago in *The Coming of Age* that confronting the reality of aging in our culture means changing the whole fabric of existence. A spirituality of aging calls in question the deepest values of our civilization. For if the aging process gradually reveals to us the mystery of life, then life's ultimate meaning cannot lie in speed, consumerism, youth, achievement, and physical beauty as currently defined by our culture. The present situation of many older people, old and young alike, has been described as a disease of the imagination. They have accepted the negative images of old age, made them their own, and begun to live out of these images of incompetence and insignificance. The task of a spirituality of aging is to convert the imaginations of both old and young to a new vision of the human. And this can only happen if the old themselves refuse to let society define them, and instead internalize new images of the later years.

The projected growth in the number of the elderly, the fact that since 1900 a quarter of a century has been added to the average life, is therefore a sign of hope. Few would argue that our current values have brought society true happiness and success. Large numbers of older people who refuse to be seduced by that value system could be an unprecedented prophetic force in the world. They could enable Christians to regain their distinct identity by declaring that our worth as human beings does not depend on our consumption and possession of things. Social analysts promise us that the elderly of the future will be more numerous, healthier, and better educated. Important as that is, the real reasons for hope lie deeper.

The task of a prophet, as the Scripture scholar Walter Brueggemann reminds us, is to offer symbols that confront a situation of hopelessness with newness.[6] By means of spoken and acted word, the prophet contradicts the presumed reality of his or her community. The prophet does this in two ways. One task of the prophet is to expose injustices which must be remedied. The elderly are prophets in this sense when they make known the suffering they experience because of destructive attitudes toward the old, inadequate income and medical care, and forced retirement at an arbitrary age. But the prophet also carries out a ministry of the imagination by proposing alternate visions of human life to a society locked into what it considers the only thinkable one. In this way a new human beginning can be made. Challenging the value system of a society requires a secure sense of who we are and the meaning that faith gives to our lives. A spirituality of aging should provide the base for late life's prophetic stance toward the world.

Keeping in mind this understanding of spirituality and the diversity that marks the later years, the following chapters will look at some of the experiences common to the last stage of the human journey, to see what light the Christian Gospel brings to them. Beneath the differences of late life lie shared concerns with dependence and independence, love and sexuality, loss, and dying, and mutual resources of wonder and contemplation, memory, humor and hope, and resurrection. A Christian perspective on these realities can begin to alter our image of aging. The prophetic work of Jesus of Nazareth was to give people a future when they believed that their present was the end, and the only possible state of existence. By his words and actions, his crucifixion and resurrection, he brought people the kind of energy that gives birth to newness.

## A Community Across Time

A spirituality of aging has importance not simply for the old. It may, in fact, be even more necessary for the young. Now that we have come to view the spiritual life not as a static state of the soul, but as movement, growth, and process, the end of the journey becomes an even more decisive influence on every stage. Like the headlight of a train moving swiftly through the night, the later years throw light on the turns and landscapes that lie ahead, preparing us for each passage. In his collection of interviews of older people, *Until the Singing Stops,* Don Gold says that he had always loved and admired his own grandmother, and that it was the memory of her that moved him to try to find others like her. He set out to meet and learn from other old people. Gold recalls that on the way to one of his interviews, he was driving along a dusty country road in Missouri and got lost. When he pulled into a farm to ask for directions, a teenager came up, listened to him, and replied, "Don't know." So he drove on. A few miles further down the road, he stopped again at a farmhouse. The farmer, a very old man, graciously gave him flawless directions. Perhaps, Gold muses, that experience summed up symbolically what he had been searching for when the memory of his grandmother sent him out looking for people like her.[7] He was looking for mentors on his life journey, knowing that such guides affect the quality of the journey for all of us. If they show us the later years of life as the fullness and deepening of earlier stages of growth, as a time of ever new discoveries of God's word, we will move toward them with confidence and hope, perhaps even with excitement and anticipation. If we see in the old only the destruction and loss of all we have known, then we will cling to our present experiences, stunting their growth by our sense that they hold no future promise.

We cannot understand any season of life unless we meditate on all of them. Spring, summer, fall, and winter stand in contrast, but in continuity. Through each of them we learn something of what it means to trust God, to love ourselves, and to love other people. What is planted in one season may not bear fruit until another; what dies in one season may emerge as the beauty of the next. Having lived through all of the seasons, older persons have a unique sense of the entire life cycle. We have become intensely aware today how interrelated our lives are in terms of space. Communication links us instantly to events around the globe, and we feel their repercussions in every corner of the world. We are just as intertwined in terms of time, though this is less clear today when there is a growing segregation of different age groups in society. How any age group, young, middle-aged, or old, faces its peculiar challenges affects all other generations. The young create hope or despair in the old; the old do the same for the young. In *Nobody Ever Died of Old Age,* Sharon Curtin recounts an old American folk tale about a wooden bowl that conveys something of this interlocking of the generations.

> It seems that Grandmother, with her trembling hands, was guilty of occasionally breaking a dish. Her daughter angrily gave her a wooden bowl, and told her that she must eat out of it from now on. The young granddaughter, observing this, asked her mother why Grandmother must eat from a wooden bowl when the rest of the family was given china plates. "Because she is old!" answered her mother. The child thought for a moment and then told her mother, "You must save the wooden bowl when Grandma dies." Her mother asked why, and the child replied, "For when you are old."[8]

Because we are all aging together, the challenges and blessings of the later years are ones we all share. We all struggle with questions of self-esteem, longing to find our ultimate worth in who we are rather than in what we do. We all know grief, loss and failure, face limitations and the final limit, death. We puzzle over our purpose in life and the lasting value of our projects. And at every age we also

stand in wonder and gratitude at the beauties of creation
and discover new dimensions of love and friendship. In
late life our questions are perhaps less theoretical and more
concrete and personal, our experiences of loss more intense
and multiple, our proximity to death more assuredly
immediate. But one of the roots of our isolation of the
elderly is our refusal to recognize the common character of
these spiritual dimensions of existence, to acknowledge our
deep similarity.

Winter grace is grace not simply for those who have
reached their later years. Older men and women can be
channels of grace and truth for all those about them. The
meaning of Christian discipleship comes clear only in the
following of Jesus. Discipleship must be learned as we
move through life and discover at each stage more of what
it means to be a Christian. There are dimensions of the
Gospel, aspects of love, courage, faith, and fidelity, which
only the old can sacramentalize for the human community.
From the perspective of faith, the later years provide the
most intense and vivid revelation of the paradox at the
heart of the Christian Gospel: that in losing our lives we
somehow find them; that loss can be gain, and weakness,
strength; that death is the path to life. Although he is not
speaking in a Christian context, D.H. Lawrence writes of
this mystery of the human person in his poem "Shadows":

> And if, in the changing phases of man's life
> I fall in sickness and in misery
> my wrists seem broken and my heart seems dead
> and strength is gone, and my life
> is only the leavings of a life:
>
> and still, among it all, snatches of lovely oblivion,
>     and snatches of renewal

odd, wintry flowers upon the withered stem, yet new,
     strange flowers
such as my life has not brought forth before, new
     blossoms of me—[9]

To be a human being is to exist between birth and death,
to be capable of both wrenching anguish and deep joy.

The Eucharist catches up in symbol this heart of the
mystery of the human. In bread and wine it celebrates both
the sacred joy of human life and the bitterness of death. In
the Eucharist, bread that is blessed and broken becomes
food for the world. Those who live to old age know the levels of brokenness that aging brings as well as the blessings
of a long life. They can deeply understand the Eucharist,
and are ready to be both challenged and consoled by it. Perhaps one of the gifts of the later years is to be Eucharist to
others, to nourish others from the riches of one's personal
experience of brokenness and blessing.

The Eucharist is meant to be an opportunity for Christians to decide what interpretation they wish to give their
lives, what values they will choose. In it the everyday experiences of our lives and the experiences of the Gospel con-
verge. The Eucharist is a Passover meal that commemo-
rates Israel's journey to freedom in the exodus, and the
freedom that comes in Jesus' death and resurrection. In late
life it can help us achieve greater distance from the values
by which society measures our worth, and new freedom to
embrace alternate ones.

The Eucharist is the deepest expression of winter grace.
It re-enacts in symbol the paradox that death somehow
leads to new life. It celebrates the unity and freedom of persons of all ages, young and old. And by recalling and making present again the paschal mystery of Christ, it reveals
the final hope that grounds this paradox.

# 2

# A HEART OF WISDOM

I met Sally one year when I was working with the elderly in downtown Seattle. She was eighty-one and lived on the streets of the city, carrying all of her possessions in a faded lavender shopping bag. Sally usually roomed at one of the missions or hotels in the old downtown area, but sometimes she slept in a doorway, bundled in newspapers or plastic to keep warm. In both winter and summer she wore oversize blue-tinted sunglasses, with which she gestured emphatically as she talked. What struck me about Sally as I got to know her was her remarkable capacity for wonder and gratitude. One day after a bingo game at the center where she often came to eat lunch, she exclaimed to me, "I won. I won." I asked her what she had chosen for a prize, hoping it was one of the items of food. "You know," she replied, "some people got canned goods or packages of rolls. But I chose this beautiful Christmas tree ornament." She held it up so that I could see its colors as they caught the afternoon sunshine through a window in the office. "Isn't it something?" she exclaimed. "I can enjoy it every day."

Later that same year Sally developed a leg problem which made it increasingly difficult for her to walk. She resisted getting medical care, but finally agreed to go with me to the downtown clinic to get a cane. The center van driver took us to within a block of the clinic, and Sally made it the rest of the way, taking painful steps and leaning on my arm. In one of the examining rooms at the clinic a nurse brought Sally a metal cane which could be expanded or contracted to various sizes. Sally was delighted, and she laughed and exclaimed excitedly as she held the cane up in the air, opening and closing it to different lengths. Then, when the nurse left the room for a moment, she turned to me and said: "I hope I haven't embarrassed you by being so happy. But I always feel such gratitude when good things happen to me. And today I received two wonderful gifts, the ride in the van and this beautiful cane." As she walked off the elevator after our visit to the clinic, Sally turned and blew me a kiss. That was the last time I saw her. She died two weeks later in a hospital in San Diego, where she had gone to get warm.

Sally remains for me a vivid example of the kind of intensity of living and rebirth of wonder possible in the later years of life. During much of our life we measure time by its duration: how many hours there are left in a day; how many days until a birthday, a holiday, a longed-for or dreaded event; how many years have passed, how many remain before us. We rush through one task in order to hasten on to the next. We use up or endure time, often squandering it like wealthy millionaires. But as we reach late life, this preoccupation with quantity gives place to an appreciation of the quality of time.[1] The slowing of our lives on several levels allows us to meet each person and situation with greater care and attentiveness. Each moment, each day, each year become more precious. We are finally able to sink into the present moment and to appreciate the ordinary things around us, to experience the depth of time as well as its duration. In *Number Our Days,* her book about a group of elderly Jews in Venice, California, anthropologist Barbara Myerhoff describes this capacity to live every aspect of life fully as one of the secrets of aging well. As one of her Jewish friends puts it: "I think this attitude you are talking about, paying such attention to life, is what we mean by 'a heart of wisdom.' In the Psalm it says, 'So teach us to number our days, that we may get us a heart of wisdom.'"[2]

Learning how to number our days means cultivating a capacity for wonder, for solitude, and for prayer. Deepening our understanding of these dimensions of the spiritual life can enrich our aging immeasurably.

### The Way to Wonder

Many older people achieve an attitude that has long been the goal of various religious traditions, a sense of the immediacy of life and a new ability to live in the present moment. Old age is a time for sorting out the more important from the less important things in life. As this happens, the elemental realities of life assume greater significance: children, plants, nature, physical and emotional touching, the textures of color and shape.[3] In his poem, "With Age Wisdom," Archibald MacLeish captures this dimension of aging.

At twenty, stooping round about,
I thought the world a miserable place,
Truth a trick, faith in doubt,
Little beauty, less grace.

Now at sixty what I see,
Although the world is worse by far,

Stops my heart in ecstasy.
God, the wonders that there are![4]

The price of this birth of wonder is an acceptance of life's limitations. Just as the lens of a camera blocks out all the other realities clamoring for our attention, letting us focus on just one thing at a time, so the discipline of acknowledging certain limits simplifies life; we see with an uncluttered vision. An older friend describes this process well in a letter.

> The eventfulness of my life has been largely my inner "events." Like noticing that the path that stretches before me has begun to slope downward in its descent into the valley where my dying waits for me. (I notice this, not morbidly, but rather with a certain amount of curiosity.) Like discovering a deeper inner peace, a large part of which, I suspect, is that I truly don't have anything left to "prove," no mountains to conquer or applause to win. In this I have been greatly blessed. . . . I have rediscovered delight in simple pleasures and a sense of time that soon forgets yesterday, gives little thought to the future, and increasingly enjoys today. I keep thinking: how *simple* it all is! Why has it taken me so long to recognize this?

Wonder is the prelude to gratitude. Once we have really taken time to see anything, it reveals the mystery of creation: we really notice for the first time the tiny rainbow a hummingbird makes or hear the first robin of spring; we catch the beauty in the face of a friend and hear the laughter of a child. Late life can be a time of deeper thanksgiving, and there are a number of simple ways to cultivate this sense of wonder and gratitude. One way is to take walks of thanksgiving. Walking is not only good exercise, but can also be an occasion for seeing and hearing the creation around us, becoming aware of its capacity to mediate the mystery of God: the first spring buds breaking on a flowering tree, the wind moving the branches of a fir tree, the sparrows hurrying about in our neighborhood. Such a walk might conclude with the praying of Psalm 104 or one of the other Psalms of thanksgiving:

> Yahweh my God, how great you are!

> You set springs gushing in ravines,
> running down between the mountains,
> supplying water for wild animals,
> attracting the thirsty wild donkeys;
> near there the birds of the air make their nests
> and sing among the branches (Ps 104, 1, 10–12).

Gardening and raising plants are other ways to increase such wonder and gratitude. Through them we observe the endless cycle of seed, plant, fruit and blossom, and stay close to the miracle of life itself.

One elderly Spanish woman whom Robert Coles interviewed in New Mexico found that simply sitting was a way to wonder.

> A few drops of rain and I feel grateful; the air is so fresh afterwards. I love to sit in the sun. We have the sun so often here, a regular visitor, a friend one can expect to see often and trust. I like to make tea for my husband and me. At midday we take our tea outside and sit on our bench, our backs against the wall of the house. Neither of us wants pillows; I tell my daughters and sons that they are soft—

those beach chairs of theirs. Imagine beach chairs here in New Mexico, so far from any ocean! The bench feels strong to us, not uncomfortable. The tea warms us inside, the sun on the outside. I joke with my husband; I say we are part of the house: the adobe gets baked and so do we. For the most part we say nothing, though. It is enough to sit and be part of God's world. We hear birds talking to each other, and are grateful they come as close to us as they do; all the more reason to keep our tongues still and hold ourselves in one place.[5]

In this silence filled with wonder and gratitude, the woman and her husband do not analyze or argue about the world; they enter into it and become one with it. They are simply resting in the real.

Such attentiveness to the wonders around us is an important form of contemplation. Contemplation is a receptive mode of awareness, the ability to really *attend* to life and take in its gifts. It has often been described as taking a long and loving look at the realities of life. To do this we must slow down a bit, or we risk trampling underfoot the delicate but inconspicuous wildflowers in a meadow, the flashes of surprise and disappointment on human faces, and the majesty of early morning sunrises. This receptive stance toward life contrasts with an active mode of aware-ness more exclusively bent on manipulating and control-ling our environment. I realized how fully this active mode can determine what we see when I was riding the bus to work one morning not long ago. It was a bitter cold day, and to the east, just behind the snow-covered peaks of the mountains, the sun was rising in a blaze of red and gold. Almost no one on the bus saw it. Some were sleeping. Oth-ers read papers from their briefcases, or scanned the morning paper. A free gift of beauty was there for the taking, and almost no one was interested.

During the course of our life we live out of both the receptive and the active modes of awareness; both are necessary. But for most of our life we work to produce and shape our environment; the active mode dominates. Later life gives us the opportunity to strengthen contemplative awareness. The late rabbi Abraham Joshua Heschel summed up this way to wonder beautifully. Several years before his death in 1972, he suffered a severe heart attack. He never fully recovered from it, and it left him very weak. To a close friend who visited him he said in a voice that was barely a whisper: "Sam, when I regained consciousness, my first feeling was not of despair or anger. I felt only gratitude to God for my life, for every moment I had lived. I was ready to depart. 'Take me, O Lord,' I thought. 'I have seen so many miracles in my lifetime.'" After a pause Heschel added: "That is what I meant when I wrote (in the preface to his book of Yiddish poems): 'I did not ask for success; I asked for wonder. And You gave it to me.'"[6]

## Prayer of the Heart

Old age is for many a time of loneliness. I remember one older woman telling me that she had a friend who had resorted to counting the lines of the wallpaper in her room in an effort to fill her hours. "I haven't come to that yet," this woman said. "But after a lifetime of work and raising a family, it is quite a challenge to fill my days." It has been suggested that the meaning of loneliness changes with age and culture. While middle-aged people in the United States see loneliness as the absence of interaction with others, for older people it often means the absence of activity. The emotional isolation experienced by many old people is a kind of boredom born of indifference. They have nothing worthwhile to do, no goals or plans: "In this, the loneliness of old people and adolescents appears to have similar roots. Both often feel isolated from other people because they have no creative outlets, no direction, no status in the busy world of adults."[7]

In the later years we are asked to value *being* over *having,* but life has not trained us well for *being.* How can we use our time to develop the interiority which is a special gift of aging? One step is to learn how to turn our loneliness into a positive season of solitude which nourishes inner freedom. The pain of loneliness can be an invitation to increase our dependence on God. At its deepest level all loneliness reflects our common experience that no created goods fully answer our inner yearnings; loneliness is rooted in a longing for God. It becomes solitude when the voice of God can be heard in its stillness. Contemplation can fill the empty silence with the reality of God's presence.

Many older people have discovered for the first time the path of prayer called centering prayer or prayer of the heart.[8] The heart is the biblical word for the center of the person, that place where God dwells and is to be found most intimately. As Paul puts it, "the love of God has been poured into our hearts by the Holy Spirit which has been given us" (Rom 5:5). Prayer of the heart is a turning to this God who loves us and is near us, the God found in our own hearts and the heart of the world. It has been described in various ways, as simply resting in the presence of God, attentive listening of the heart, waiting for God. Thomas Merton says it is "finding one's deepest center, awakening the profound depths of our being in the presence of God who is the source of our being and our life."[9]

Learning how to pray in this way is not difficult. Most writers on prayer agree that there are certain steps which prepare us for such prayer by opening us to God's presence. Traditional works on prayer often speak of a kind of discipline or emptying as a prelude to this prayer. One of the reasons that prayer of the heart is very natural for many older people is that this emptying has already taken place as a result of the process of aging; it has stripped us of many possessions and preoccupations which muffle the voice of God. Aging also slows us down and gives us more solitude and time for prayer. The other side of the emptying of aging is the fullness found in the contemplative presence of God. It prepares us for that communion which, in the Christian vision, is what death brings.

Prayer comes only as a gift; what we do is ready ourselves for the gift. All the techniques we read about are really ways of bringing ourselves to that stillness where the voice of God can be heard. Part of this readiness is setting aside a regular time for prayer. In *The Desert Blooms: A Personal Adventure in Growing Old Creatively,* Sarah-Patton Boyle emphasizes the importance of such spiritual routines. When the structures of her previous roles were removed, she thought that she would revel in the new freedom and creativity. Instead, she felt like a door that had been taken off its hinges. Without her previous connections with a frame, she expected to be able to swing freely in all directions, but instead she could only lean stiffly against the wall. She reflects later:

> Wiser now, I saw that if I had established spiritual routines, my present life would not be devoid of familiar grooves. I would have a comfortable, supporting structure from which to deal with the drastic changes and dislocations I had met. Spiritual routines can be followed continuously from childhood through old age. Largely independent of

both circumstances and human relationships, they are almost indestructible from outside. They ensure an enduring nucleus to sustain us under all conditions. Secure in them we can cope successfully with outer destruction. Establishing spiritual grooves in which to relax and gather strength may well be the greatest need of our day.[10]

In addition to this routine or set time, a set place is helpful for our prayer. Anyone who has ever struggled with sickness, loneliness or loss knows how important structuring one's day can be. Such structures or familiar grooves direct our energies and create a sense of personal order and purpose.

Posture is also important. Bodily posture is a way of expressing our total self in prayer. Certain postures also make it easier to pray. A common element in the suggestions made by the great religious traditions is that the spine be straight and the body comfortably relaxed but alert. This enables us to breathe in a deep and relaxed way, and yet not easily doze off into sleep. Many of the postures learned in yoga also prepare us for prayer. Usually it is helpful to close our eyes. Another way of coming to the relaxed alertness that readies us for prayer is to concentrate on our breathing, breathing in and out deeply several times. As we breathe out, we can breathe away all our fears and worries, and then breathe in the love and life of God. All of these preparations are meant to provide a quieting time which opens us to God's love.

Entry into centering prayer can begin with the slow, loving recitation of the lines of a favorite Psalm or the words of the Our Father. Any short prayer form repeated over and over again slowly and quietly can help to still our spirit. Some forms of the prayer of the heart use a single word like "Jesus" or "God," or a short ejaculation such as "Come, Lord. Come, Lord Jesus." Whenever we become aware that we are focusing on other things during the prayer, we gently return to this word or phrase. The rosary has been the path into contemplative prayer for many older people, and it can be a very rich form of prayer. It is a familiar prayer, and therefore it is possible to move beyond the words into a quiet awareness of God. That is why forgetting the words, or realizing that we have moved from attention to them to presenting our concerns to God or just being with God in prayer, should be no cause for worry. Nor should failure to finish the rosary. The rosary beads are a concrete, physical way of grounding our prayer and attention; they enflesh our words, making then tangible. Because many have prayed the rosary often during their life, it is a symbol that catches up past and present. The repetition of its phrases can lead to an attentive heart.

In the depth of our solitude we will discover other people. Solitude is primarily a quality of the heart, not a place, and it always has social dimensions. The former editor of *America,* John LaFarge, puts it this way: "In our later years we become more conscious that we do not pray alone. The Church is praying with us and in us—the whole Mystical Body of Christ."[11] Noises and concerns, what we sometimes call distractions, are simply reminders that we never pray for ourselves alone. We can lift each of these persons and concerns to God as they come into our awareness. We may think that prayer means setting aside all else in order to think only about God; thoughts or feelings that are not pious or religious are distractions. However, prayer is a loving relationship with God which catches up all of life, not just a part of it. God is even more concerned than we are with every aspect of our lives: relationships with our families, new friendships, financial worries, physical pain.

We cannot judge the value of our prayer by the way we feel during it. If we open ourselves to a relationship with God, it will affect all our life. Prayer may be hard for us; sometimes we feel that God is far away and nothing is happening. What we may often find, however, is that after prayer we have more strength and hope. The real test of any prayer is the quality of our Christian life: growth in trust in God and ourselves, the kind of trust that was so characteristic of Jesus; greater love for others, a broadening of our love to include all those in need, and a willingness to forgive; less fear of what others may think of us and a greater freedom to be ourselves.

Prayer of the heart is central to a positive pattern of aging in yet another way. In such contemplation, we do not reason about this or that dogma of faith. Rather, we seek the deepest ground of our identity in God. We discover who we are and why we exist. We experience the truths of faith, especially the simple presence of God, in our own life. When life becomes difficult for us in the later years, we may be tempted to fall into a kind of prayer that becomes more and more an asking of God for what we think will bring us out of our difficulties. Many older people say to me, "I don't think even God cares about me. I pray and pray and nothing happens." Prayer of the heart consists not so much in letting God know again and again what we need, as in a deepening of our capacity to hear what God wants of us, in simple listening to God's purpose revealed in the depth of our own hearts and of reality. In contemplation we do not simply prepare for a certain kind of message that we want to hear. We remain expectant, knowing that we can never really anticipate the word which will turn our darkness into light. In this process we sometimes learn for the first time what our own deepest concerns are. The greatest realization that may come is that God loves our real selves, the angry, lonely, or depressed persons we are, not the ideal selves we would like to be. We need not hide our feelings of anger, sexuality, guilt, or worthlessness from God. They are all part of coming to God in prayer just as we are, to be loved for no other reason than that we *are.*

Prayer is a nurturing of our relationship with God, and it can take many forms: vocal prayers, listening to a favorite hymn, a review of our day before God, dance, prayers of petition or intercession, or group prayer which provides a way of reaching out to others. Prayer of the heart is one path which has been helpful to many in their later years. Through such prayer we learn that relating to God is not necessarily a matter of saying many words; often it is simply resting in the presence of God, aware that God is in us and we are in God.

## Praying with Scripture

Many also find it helpful to pray with Scripture. There are many ways to pray with the Bible. One helpful method is to begin by selecting a passage from Scripture that is one of your favorites. It is best to keep the passage short, perhaps five to ten verses. Once you have chosen a section from the Bible, find a place of solitude and spend a few moments quieting yourself in the ways suggested above. Then recall that you are in God's presence, and ask for the grace to be open to God's word.

Read the passage from Scripture very slowly and listen carefully and peacefully to it. You may want to read it out loud. Do not try to look for implications or lessons, or to develop profound thoughts about it. Just let God's word in the passage sink in slowly. When something strikes you, do not hurry to move on. Savor the word or phrase that speaks to you. Some words may carry special meaning for you or puzzle you. But do not get discouraged if you think nothing is happening. Listening is itself a prayer. Pray whatever prayers arise in you. These may be prayers of thanksgiving, of discouragement, of longing, need, joy, or confusion.

Throughout the centuries this kind of contemplative praying of the Scriptures has been called *lectio divina,* or sacred reading. In *Daily We Touch Him. Practical Religious Experiences,* M. Basil Pennington summarizes a simple method for such reading: (1) Rule One: Take the text with reverence and call upon the Holy Spirit; (2) Rule Two: For ten minutes we listen to the Lord and respond to him; (3) Rule Three: Take a word with thanksgiving.[12] These first two rules summarize what we have said about beginning with the presence of God and then listening slowly to God speaking to you in the words of the passage. In his third rule Pennington is suggesting that you choose a word from all that you have heard, and carry it with you. This allows your prayer time to spill over into the rest of your day. Some days you will have heard a particular word with such power that it will abide with you for days: "Courage! It is I! Do not be afraid" (Mk 6:51); "Happy the peacemakers: they shall be called children of God" (Mt 5:9). At other times you may have to choose a word to keep with you.

Another helpful way to contemplate a passage is to enter imaginatively into it. Insert yourself into the scene and become one of the people present with Jesus. See the surroundings, hear the words, and let God touch you in this way. For example, in John 4:1–42 you might become the Samaritan woman Jesus meets at the well. Feel the roughness of the bucket and the cool water as you go to draw from the well. Hear Jesus asking you "Give me a drink." Sense your own deep thirst for a water that will last, and recall all the places you have gone in search of such water. Hear Jesus tell you that he will still this deeper thirst you have for life and salvation by giving you living water: "Whoever drinks this water will get thirsty again; but anyone who drinks the water I shall give will never be thirsty again." What are you feeling as he speaks these words? Jesus also sends you back to your own people, restores you to the human community: "Many Samaritans of that town had believed in him on the strength of the woman's testimony when she said, 'He told me all I have ever done.'" Who are these people in your life? Enter as fully into the passage as you can, so that its power can reach you on all levels. You can do the same with many other passages. For instance, you might become the man born blind who becomes able to see again in John 9:1–41 or one of the guests invited to the wedding in Luke 14:15–24.

Contemplation of the Gospels is especially important as we grow older because our lives no longer conform easily to those of a society that prizes speed, youth, efficiency, and productivity. Praying with the Scriptures keeps alive another vision of what human life is meant to be and how it should be lived, one built on the values Jesus came to teach us: love, courage, peace, forgiveness, and joy.

## Wisdom Is Someone

When questioned about the areas of progress that come with aging, most people respond that aging brings growth in wisdom. But exactly what is meant by this nod toward wisdom is difficult to determine. Wisdom is an elusive quality. To many older people it connotes a superior knowledge of some kind, and they say they do not have it. In fact, they find its attribution a burden, because they believe they must muster a degree of expertise they do not really believe they possess.

Certain biblical traditions reflect this notion of wisdom as a kind of knowledge based on experience. Wisdom is sage advice for the young, and practical suggestions for coping with the world. Wisdom often took the form of wise sayings of parents to children or of teachers to students: "A good name is more desirable than great wealth, the respect of others is better than silver or gold" (Prv 22:1). Later books probe more deeply the origins of Wisdom. Job 28 is a piece of poetry that asks:

> But Wisdom, where is Wisdom to be found?
> Where is the hiding place of understanding? (12)

After a series of non-answers to this crucial question, the poem continues:

> God is the One who understands the way to Wisdom,
> the One acquainted with its hiding place. (23)

It is God who gives our life and universe its meaning. But this Wisdom is still a principle, a something, and not yet a someone with whom human beings can relate. In Proverbs 1:20-23, however, Wisdom is no longer spoken *of*. Rather, Wisdom speaks for herself; Wisdom is not something, but someone: "Whoever listens to me may live secure; they will have quiet, fearing no mischance" (33).

Wisdom is God's gift. How, then, do I become wise? Not simply by learning more about life and readying myself with sage advice for the young. Wisdom comes from contact with God. The fruits of this communion are the wonder and gratitude found in living each moment fully, the love and freedom learned in solitude and prayer. The sharing of this wisdom is not primarily in terms of what we say or do for the young, but through the persons we have become. At bottom, winter grace is the entry of God into our lives, a coming that gives us a heart of wisdom.

*3*

# MEMORIES

The fear of forgetting and the need to remember both mark the later years of life. This fear and need spring from the same truth. Memory is more than a resource for efficient living or a reservoir of colorful and entertaining stories. Memory enables us to hold fast to our identity and shape it in new ways. Beneath the annoyance we experience at not being able to recall names and dates or find our glasses is the nagging fear that some part of us is slipping away. On the other hand, remembering events and people from our past lets us claim and share our selves. Somewhere within us still lives the girl of nine racing across the grass in the summer sunshine, the young man finding his way in first friendships, the wife receiving the news of her husband's fatal heart attack. We do not merely *have* these memories; we *are* these memories. Western culture tends to view time as more destructive than creative. But memory is a way of describing the cumulative nature of time, the presence of the past within us. Time not only unravels; it also knits up.

Not only is memory fundamental to personal identity; it is central to religious identity. Memory reveals God's presence in our life. Memories retrace a sacred journey. Some older adults in a poetry reading group made this point movingly for me. One of them had brought a poem called "The House Where I Was Born" to a session. As we discussed the poem, a woman in her early nineties told us that her own mother had died in childbirth, so she had never really known her. But she remembered the little house where she had lived with her father and stepmother. When she was eight years old, her stepmother became very ill, and she still remembered vividly her father's hoarse voice calling from her stepmother's bedside, "She's gone." As the woman shared these memories, tears welled up in her eyes, and she began to cry. We were all silent, realizing how present that moment from eighty years past was to her. Then I said to her, "Those are painful memories." She stopped crying, looked up, and almost defiantly replied: "Those are *sacred* memories." The woman next to her added, "They are *holy* memories. We need such memories."

How are our memories holy and sacred? In this chapter we will look at four aspects of the religious meaning of memory: (1) memory and religious identity, (2) the joyful mysteries of our lives, (3) the healing of memories, and (4) ritual as a way to remember.

## Memory and Religious Identity

The Hebrew Scriptures speak of the old as "full of days." This phrase captures the deepest meaning of remembering, for as the philosopher Alfred North Whitehead tells us, memory is really another word for presence. Events that are finished live on in the very constitution of our being; we *are* all that we have experienced, even though we may not be able to remember or be conscious of all that has affected us. We are indeed full of days. The relationships we have had during our lifetime, for example, have not been simply passing external occurrences. They are essential to our becoming; they have entered into the fabric of our lives. The past is not, as we sometimes think, slipping away and distancing itself from us. Rather, it is piling up, constitutive of the present. That is why remembering is so basic to an enduring sense of self-worth. It is a search for a self to be and to love.

Many older people spend time gathering together the materials that compose their lives. Some put their life story in writing as a gift for future family generations. Others reread old letters, page through scrapbooks, or visit important sites from their childhood or growing years. For others, the gathering is much more informal, triggered perhaps by an old song that causes characters from the past to crowd in on them. A friend in her seventies and I were taking a walk one November evening after dinner. An early fog was settling into the trees and the tops of the light posts. As we turned the corner toward home she looked up at the white puffs of fog against one of the street lights and said, "When I see that, I am all at once back again in Minnesota as a girl. I remember dad getting out the sleigh, bundling us up, and heading out across the snow. I feel happy all over again when I recall those times." This power of things to trigger memories is one reason why familiar objects are so important to us as we grow older. Others may urge us to get rid of an old desk or chair and replace it with a newer model. But we know that with it will go a lifetime of memories. As one woman expressed it, "You remember when you turned to it when you needed to cry, and when you needed to laugh." Symbols can, in fact, bear in concentrated form the meanings of years and generations of experience.

Whether it happens formally or informally, this recollecting is one way of possessing ourselves, of saying, "This is who I am." Writing in her eighties, Florida Scott-Maxwell sums up this process well: "You need only claim the events of your life to make yourself yours. When you truly possess all you have been and done, which may take some time, you are fierce with reality. When at last age has assembled you together, will it not be easy to let it all go, lived, balanced, over?"[1] Remembering is a way of finding the pattern or design of our lives, the shape which makes each life experience unique and gives it meaning. This pattern, relating part to part, and part to whole, gives significance to otherwise meaningless experiences. That is why as we grow older we try to piece together a unified self from all the fragments of our lives.

During recent decades this experience of remembering has become a focus of interest among professionals working with older adults. Robert N. Butler, a psychiatrist who has written extensively on topics related to aging, believes that the experience of reviewing one's life is universal among older people.[2] Butler sees life review as a looking back which is set in motion by looking forward to death. It accounts for the increased reminiscing which he believes characterizes the later years. The process of reviewing our lives can result in increased candor, serenity, and wisdom. It can lead to the expiation of guilt, the reconciliation of relationships, and the resolution of inner conflicts. But recalling unresolved conflicts or past inadequacies can also lead to depression, anxiety, and a sense that our lives have been a waste. Erik Erikson believes that such failure to accept one's life cycle leads to fear of death and a despair that will often be expressed in disgust. This disgust is basically lack of acceptance of oneself, but it often finds voice in chronic complaining and disgust with everything. A faith perspective is crucial if remembering is indeed to result in integrity and peace.

For faith adds an essential dimension to our remembering. In faith we not only gather our memories; we recollect our lives before God. Our stories then take on new meaning as part of a larger story which embraces and redeems them. Such remembering is the biblical way of appropriating the past, and the basis of religious identity. At each key juncture in her life, Israel retold the story of what God had done for her, how God had remained faithful in the midst of her infidelities, how God's presence had sustained her in times of trial. By remembering she made God's love present again with power. Out of these memories arose new courage and hope that God's promises would again be fulfilled. Like Israel we also tell and retell our stories, since they have levels of meaning which cannot be completely captured in a single telling.

This way of remembering is a confession of faith. As Amos Wilder has said, when a Christian of any time or place confesses his or her faith, this confession turns into a story.[3] Maria, an older woman in one of my theology classes, confirmed this truth. When asked to write about the meaning of faith, she gave us the gift of her life story. It was a recollection of her life before God. Maria had been born in the Netherlands and lived there until she was twenty-nine. One part of her story describes life after she and her husband moved to America.

> One day there came a telegram from the Netherlands. It read: "Father seriously sick." The next day another telegram: "Father died peacefully." It felt like a bomb had fallen in our little world and shattered it all to pieces. We could not go back; we had to stay in this land we had freely chosen, live among people we did not understand, neither were understood by.

> That evening I was brought to the hospital and lost our baby, a miscarriage. I could fold my hands

and close my eyes but no words, no thoughts, only emptiness—silence. I did not search for communion with God. He seemed so far. Our family had said when we left: "Remember, there are planes. You can come back, you are not in a concentration camp." And now, at this time, I wanted to go back, but I could not, even though there were planes. It was not that simple.

Yet, God restores and heals. We experienced this in the fullest measure. We lived for two years on the prairie. We had a large garden and ate all that it provided. We saved almost every penny, we were so longing to leave the hog ranch. Every evening, we went through the garbage for glass milk and cream bottles. These we sold in the little country store and in turn were able to buy bananas and oranges for the little girl God gave us one year after my miscarriage.

As Maria shows us in her life story, faith is the recounting of God's presence in our journey through time. This is especially true as we age and experience our temporality more fully. The only way to capture a self extended over time is through story. And only the old can know in their own lives how an entire life cycle is a revelation of God.

When individuals share their journeys of faith, they move closer to community. These stories reveal our individual uniqueness, the particular circumstances and decisions that have shaped each of us. But they do more. They lay bare universal realities, our common fears and joys. As we listen to the story of another unfold, we often find ourselves saying, "Yes, I have had that same experience." We realize that we are not alone in the universe; there are others like us.

As we grow older, we may find it more difficult to recall details like names and dates. But often we can remember key moments of our past lives: events and decisions which profoundly changed us, riches which different friends brought to us, difficulties we conquered and successes we achieved, griefs and joys we have known. These moments are finally more important than the details we find ourselves forgetting. Recollecting these larger dimensions of our lives before God can strengthen not only our identity and self-worth, but our awareness of God's presence with us.

## The Joyful Mysteries of Our Lives

By entering into past occasions of grace and joy, we experience again the gift of God's love and healing. Biblical remembering is not simply "living in the past." The Hebrew verb "to remember" means bringing the past into the present in such a way that it influences present decisions and conduct. Memory is often an untapped reservoir of comfort and peace. Tapping that reservoir is one way of praying the joyful mysteries of our lives. There are more than five joyful mysteries, even though that is the number we associate with praying the rosary. There are as many joyful mysteries as there are experiences of God's grace in our lives. But we sometimes have to make time in our day to focus quite deliberately on these joyful memories. We seem to return more easily to painful ones.

Open the album of your life. There you will find scenes in which you felt deeply loved or in which you knew joy: a wedding day, your family together for a holiday, your birthday celebrated with friends. Choose one of these joyful mysteries of your life. Take some time to recapture the original scene and the feelings that accompanied it. How was this love shown to you? By whom? What produced the joy in you? Call up the scene again in detail, and let yourself experience some of the love and joy you felt when the event first took place. The work of memory is not simply recalling old dates, names, and places. It is the reawakening of those moments. Simply to feel again the feeling, here and now, is healing. In feeling and imagination we are all the ages we have ever been. An older man described such an experience. "Most of the time," he said, "I go back to the bad memories, like the times I failed. When I think about them, I feel bad about myself. One morning I didn't think I could face the day. So I went back over some of the times my wife told me good things about myself. It was as if she were saying them to me again. Afterward, I felt stronger inside."

Rather than choosing one scene, you may wish to pray over many scenes in your life and open your heart to the gifts of God found there. Perhaps you remember a family fishing trip, and thank God for graces of joy and renewal. A scene at work calls to mind past struggles and fears and you realize that the God who was with you then is with you now. You recall friends who came into your life, perhaps only briefly, and thank God that they remain forever a part of you.

Exercises such as these can do several things. They make our own some of the experiences we moved through too quickly to fully grasp. In her short story, "I Stand Here Ironing," Tillie Olsen describes the difficulty many of us know: "And when is there time to remember, to sift, to weigh, to estimate, to total? I will start and there will be an interruption and I will have to gather it all together again. Or I will become engulfed with all I did or did not do, with what should have been and what cannot be helped."[4] It takes time to appropriate the religious meaning of events. Praying the joyful mysteries of our lives lets us unwrap each gift of life slowly, and perhaps appreciate it fully for the first time. It brings revised and expanded understanding of these events, and allows us to piece together our own faith history.

Such memories allow us to experience the fact that God loves us. Feelings of worthlessness often accompany aging in our society. Self-worth, we are told, should be rooted in God's love for us. But it is not enough simply to hear these words. We need to relive events that mediate God's graciousness to us. Joyful memories are a sacrament of that love.

In *The Sacred Journey,* Frederick Buechner stresses that we can continue to learn from all of our memories. Memory, he says, is not the looking back to a past that no longer exists. Rather, it allows us to look into an altogether new kind of time where everything that ever was continues to be. Something of the power and richness of life continues to touch us through the people we loved and who loved us, the people who taught us things: "Dead and gone though they may be, as we come to understand them in new ways, it is as though they come to understand us—and through them we come to understand ourselves—in new ways too."[5] This, Buechner believes, is something of the meaning of the communion of saints.

## The Healing of Memories

Our lives all contain sorrowful as well as joyful mysteries. Some older people do not want to remember the past because it contains too many painful memories and unresolved conflicts. But how we view the past affects profoundly how we live the present. Regret, hurt, and guilt over the past contribute to the bitterness some older people feel toward life. A denial of failures can set up divisions within us, absorbing our springs of energy. Awareness of sins committed in the past or of opportunities for grace left unfulfilled may make us afraid to die. As one older woman told me, "I said to God, 'Don't call me yet; I'm too dirty to go.'" The healing of memories is therefore a major grace of the later years.

This healing of memories is part of the ongoing biblical journey. Like other events in her history, the exodus story mirrors Israel's capacity not only for fidelity, but also for betrayal. She murmurs against the hardships in the desert. She turns for security to a golden calf. If she is to continue her journey she must forgive herself and accept God's forgiveness for her failures. So must we. Such healing and forgiveness are essential if wisdom rather than despair is to mark the later years.

A story from the biblical wisdom literature recounts such a healing of memories. It is the tale of Joseph found in Genesis 37–50. As the Jewish scholar Samuel Sandmel says, in this long and complicated story "we follow Joseph from priggish adolescence, through misadventure, temptation, and ordeal, into triumph and magnanimity."[6] The story of Joseph is well known. The favorite of his father Jacob, Joseph so alienates his brothers that they sell him into slavery in Egypt and report to Jacob that Joseph has died. Later, when famine makes it necessary for Jacob and his sons to look for food, ten of the sons travel to Egypt to make purchases. Joseph has by now risen to second in command in Egypt. He recognizes his brothers, but they do not recognize him. After several tricks and ruses, Joseph reveals himself to them, forgives them for the deed they unjustly did him in the past, and locates his family near him in Egypt. Elie Wiesel says of Joseph, "When he suc-

ceeded in vanquishing his bitterness and eventually transforming it into inspiration and love, he became a recon-
ciled, happy man. At peace with his father, his brother, his
neighbors, his subjects."[7]

This wisdom story is the pattern of all paths to wisdom. We escape despair through the healing and forgiveness of past memories. Well into their seventies and eighties some persons continue to cling to pain and anger from
mistakes they believe their parents made in raising them.
Or they experience regret and guilt over the way their own
children have turned out. They may remain unwilling to
forgive a friend or relative for a past hurt they experienced.
Deep within them bitterness festers, eating away at the
peace and supportive relationships so essential to happiness in the later years. When he was eighty-two, the long-
time editor of *America,* John LaFarge, S. J., wrote an essay
"On Turning Seventy." In it he speaks of old age as preem-
inently the time of reparation. Old age, he says, is a time of
prayer, love and courage, and all three enter into that great
work of reparation. Though we cannot turn back the clock
of time, with the help of God we can rewrite our lives and
even rewrite the lives of others.[8] The meaning of our past
changes as we change. Another John, Pope John XXIII,
drew up a final spiritual testament nearly a decade before
his death in 1963. He was seventy-three at the time, and in
it he asks forgiveness from all those whom he has unknow-
ingly offended, and from those whom he has not influenced
for good.[9]

The healing of memories depends on recognizing that
there is no point in life too late for God's call to new life.
The theory that older people are set in their ways and cannot change has finally been exposed for the harmful stereotype that it is. In fact, the later years create a special readiness for conversion. We no longer have the physical energy

necessary to support resentments and conflicts, and we are less willing to spend our energy on things that do not matter. We have experienced more of life and are often ready to recognize our own limitations. We are facing the end of our lives and know that opportunities for healing and reconciliation are dwindling. For all these reasons the later years are times of special receptivity to God's healing of our unfinished stories.

In their many writings on the healing of memories, Dennis and Matthew Linn provide helpful insights on this dimension of aging.[10] They stress that two dispositions are essential to healing the past. The first is a willingness to become forgiving and let go of bitterness. One help in reaching this readiness to forgive is to try to see the persons who have offended us in their own contexts. What personal suffering, past experiences, or lack of knowledge might have contributed to their actions? This attitude was expressed in Jesus' prayer from the cross: "Father, forgive them; they do not know what they are doing" (Lk 23:34). The second disposition for healing is the capacity to see the past in a new and positive light, to believe that even painful experiences can be gifts. We are apt to see only the dark side of the past, but God can help us find the beneficial aspects of our personal hurts, so that in the end we can find something to be thankful for even in them.

Many of our gifts in fact developed during what seemed to be tragic moments in our past. We may have lost most of our material possessions in the 1929 Depression, but in the process discovered new inner strength or family bonds. Perhaps we endured a prolonged illness, but experienced during it the support and love of friends. Here is how one older woman described the way she learned to forgive her husband who left her for another woman when she still had two small children to raise: "I had so many experiences and did so many things I never would have done. It's like so many of what seem to be the very worst things in your life. When you flip the page, you find that they contained the seeds of what turn out to be some of the very best things in your life." Time and distance are necessary for such perspective and healing. That is why wisdom is ascribed to old age. We have then lived long enough to view our tragedies in the context of a whole life and to see not only what we have lost, but the ways in which we were enriched.

If we cannot see how a painful memory opened us to God, our neighbor, or our self, we may need to return to that memory in prayer. In *Sadhana* Anthony De Mello suggests a way of doing this.

> Return to some scene in the past where you have felt pain or grief or hurt or fear or bitterness. . . . Relive the event. . . . But this time seek and find the presence of the Lord in it. . . . In what way is he present there?. . .
>
> Or, imagine that the Lord himself is taking part in the event. . . . What role is he playing? . . . Speak to him. Ask him the meaning of what is happening. . . . Listen to what he says in reply. . . .[11]

When beginning this kind of prayer it is necessary to take some time to relax in the way suggested in Chapter II for centering prayer. Then we need to really enter the event in our imagination, watching and listening to what is happening, and dialoguing out with God whatever is in our hearts until we are satisfied. Such prayer is not a matter of stirring up past painful memories which we have resolved and forgotten. It is, rather, a way of dealing with those memories which still need the gift of God's healing because they are barriers to our present peace and happiness. Prayer puts these memories in the context of faith.

Often as we attempt to round out our lives in the later years, we find that we need to forgive ourselves. Such forgiveness is part of accepting the forgiveness and healing of God. We have hurt others during our lifetime, intentionally and unintentionally. Our children are not perfect; we made mistakes in bringing them up. We missed opportunities and so settled for less than we might have been. We are as conscious of what we might have done as of what we actually did. Growing old requires the acceptance of the unfulfilled. As the poet Gerard Manley Hopkins says, we need to be gentle with our own limitations.

> My own heart let me more have pity on; let
> Me live to my sad self hereafter kind, charitable . . .
> Leave comfort root-room.[12]

As Christians we know that our stories are embraced and redeemed by the larger story of Jesus. That story is above all a parable of God's love and mercy. If God has so forgiven us, we must be ready to forgive ourselves. Wisdom and wholeness come, as Erik Erikson reminds us, from the ability to accept our one and only life cycle.[13] Jesus helps us to do it, if we walk through our life cycle with him. *He* accepts it. Forgiveness is also a way of sharing in the redemption of the world. When we forgive, we give others the possibility of relating to us and to others in a new way, free of the hurt that lack of forgiveness brings. They are changed by our forgiveness; it expands the power of Christ's healing in the world.

## Ritual as a Way To Remember

Symbolic action or ritual is a fundamental way of remembering. Exodus 13:9–10 speaks of the way ritual can help us remember. The Passover ritual will serve, it says, as a sign on our hand or a memento on our forehead would, to remind us how God brought us out of Egypt. Ritual allows us to express the deepest emotional levels of our memories, and it is therefore especially important at times of joy and celebration, as well as loss and death. An experience at a senior center where I worked made me realize how difficult it is for older adults to deal with multiple losses when there are few rituals available to them. Three regular members of our center died within a few days of one another. One died in another city and word of his death came by mail. Another was struck by a car while crossing an intersection during a heavy Sunday evening rain storm. The third had had a massive heart attack. As word of the deaths came, members struggled to handle their grief. Many had no familiar rituals to turn to for help.

One man, Pete, responded by creating his own simple ritual of grieving. He wanted somehow to remember Margaret, the woman who had died of a heart attack. Margaret frequently baked cookies to share with the center members, and arrived early to set out coffee for them. Pete lived in a downtown hotel and his only income was a small monthly social security check. He usually ate breakfast at one of the fast food restaurants lining the street near his hotel. He told me that the morning after Margaret's death he had watched people on their way to work as they stopped in the restaurant to buy lottery tickets. Then an idea came to him. He would use his money to buy something more important than a lottery ticket—a bag of cookies to share with the center members. As he recounted this, he pointed to the cookies on a table nearby. With them was a sign he had made: "In memory of Margaret." "I thought it might mean something to her," he said. Then he took my hand and began to cry. The ritual enabled Pete to express realities which were in many ways incommunicable. Through ritual, memories and connections are invoked, as it were, inside our skins.

As is clear from the memorial Pete created, rituals need not be elaborate. A simple ceremony with Scripture readings and prayers can be prepared when someone is retiring from work or leaving a lifelong home for a new living situation. Lighted candles can also be used. Stories, blessings, and symbols such as pictures and cherished mementos also contribute to effective rituals.

Ritual is important because it provides a sense of continuity, a link not just with our individual past, but with that of our culture and our faith. The noted anthropologist Barbara Myerhoff makes clear in her delightful book *Number Our Days* what a central role ritual can play in the life of older people. Spending time at the Aliyah Senior Citizens' Center in Venice, California, Dr. Myerhoff learned how rituals like birthday celebrations, funerals and memorials developed these elderly Jews' identity, affirmed their basic beliefs and values, and preserved their continuity with the past. The Oneg Shabbat ceremony celebrated on Fridays at the Center evoked early memories for many, as it did for a Center woman named Basha.

> Do you know what it meant to me when I was called to the candles last Friday? I'll tell you. When I was a little girl, I would stand this way, beside my mother when she would light the candles for Shabbat. We were alone in the house, everything warm and clean and quiet with all the good smells of the cooking food coming in around

us. We were still warm from the mikva. My braids very tight, to last through Shabbes, made with my best ribbons. Whatever we had, we wore our best. To this day, when the heat of the candles is on my face, I circle the flame and cover my eyes, and then I feel again my mother's hands on my smooth cheeks.[14]

The enactment of ancient rituals brings renewed awareness of where we have come from and who we are. It can help us establish profound emotional connections in terms of our identities as individuals and members of families. In this way we capture the feeling of an old self or a partial self. Ritual is one of the paths to integrity as we age.

As Christians we are asked to reenact such an ancient ritual in Jesus' memory. The Eucharist is a memorial meal. And like the central celebrations of the Jewish faith, this ritual commemoration is more than a mere remembrance of a past happening. It puts us in touch not just with a memory, but with a living presence. In the Eucharist our memories are taken up into the paschal mystery of Christ; there we experience a healed past and a transformed future. The Eucharist celebrates and makes present the central elements that are part of all of our remembering: the love of God experienced in our life stories, the reconciliation of sinners in Christ's body, the healing and forgiveness that come to us through Christ.

The Eucharist as memorial also reminds us that memory is a sacrament of hope. The Eucharistic liturgy remembers the past, but this memory bears a promise. The Eucharist points to a "day of the Lord" yet to come. As we enter again into the death/resurrection mystery of Jesus, we realize that true remembering contains hope for the future and helps us move into that future.

# 4

# DEPENDENCE AND INDEPENDENCE

One of the things we fear most about old age is increased dependence on others. This dependence can take many forms. An older friend of mine had lived happily in a downtown hotel for several years until she fell and broke her hip. After her release from the hospital, she moved in with her daughter for several weeks. "I feel like such a burden," she said. "I just try to stay out of her way as much as I can." Another man in his seventies described to me the day he had to lay down his car keys because problems with low vision and arthritis made it unsafe for him to drive: "After all these years of driving others places, I now find it almost impossible to ask them to take me someplace." Learning to deal with issues of dependence and independence is a major challenge of aging. Moreover, it is one of the aspects of aging most in need of a Christian perspective. For our culture has distorted the meaning of both dependency and autonomy, and in doing so it has put in peril not only the experience of aging, but human community as well.

While growing up, we learn to prize independence very highly. Babies and children can lean on others for support and sustenance, but anyone of adult age who has to depend

51

on others is inferior. We tell ourselves: "Stand on your own two feet." "Do it yourself; don't bother anybody with it." This conviction that adults should be able to take care of themselves applies especially to finances, but it extends to most other areas of life as well. We should be able to manage our own households and get around by ourselves. Independence expresses our desire to preserve control over our lives and to affirm our own and others' freedom. This emphasis on self-reliance and individual autonomy results in disapproval of dependency in ourselves and in others. Throughout much of our adult life we ignore the many kinds of dependence that bind us to others.

Society's positive evaluation of independence and its negative attitude toward dependency create anxiety and fear among older adults when illness, poverty, or failing hearing or sight increases their need for help. One study found that financial and physical dependency was the principal cause of low morale among older people.[1] Such dependence can increase the vulnerability of the elderly and the risk of exploitation. An older person's dependence on adult children can strain a relationship since both parent and child may feel guilt and resentment about the new situation. Some older people would literally rather die than become dependent. Since independence is a criterion for self-worth, many elderly ask themselves, "Will I be of any worth as a person if I can no longer do everything for myself?"

Problems arise when we regard any dependence as degrading and so cling to a rigid and desperate notion of independence which blocks out human friendship and even endangers our life. Problems also arise when well-meaning friends and relatives equate aging with lack of competence and preempt decisions which we are still capable of making for ourselves. When others imply that we are so much less than they are that we can never make it without their help. our confidence falls apart. The right to think and act for oneself is essential to human dignity. When our right to make decisions concerning our own welfare is not recognized, we feel that our humanness has been bypassed; we experience ourselves as isolated from the human race. This saps our energy and engenders despair.

What light can Christian faith bring to this central dimension of aging, the relationship between dependence and independence? It can free us from a false dichotomy between them, enabling us instead to affirm the freedom of each person while at the same time recognizing the dependencies which are part of every mature lifestyle. The Christian vision is of an *interdependent* community of persons who are all both weak and strong in various ways, and who mutually exchange their gifts. Such a community recognizes the interdependence of the generations in the ongoing process of life. In the next sections we will explore the meaning and practical consequences of this vision for an understanding of aging: (1) interdependence in Christ, (2) receiving as a way of loving, and (3) baptism into Jesus' death and resurrection.

## Interdependence in Christ

In his letter to the Christians in Galatia Paul says that belief in Christ means a whole new way of relating to others. He quotes what is probably a baptismal fragment from an early Christian liturgy: "All baptized in Christ, you have all clothed yourselves in Christ, and there are no more distinctions between Jew and Greek, slave and free, male and female, but all of you are one in Christ Jesus" (Gal 3:27–28). If Paul were living today, he might add "young and old" to his list. For what Paul is telling the Galatians is that no one is free unless all enjoy the freedom of Christ together.

A central conviction in the New Testament is that the Kingdom of God has already broken into history, transforming the old social order. Now, by virtue of baptism in Christ, distinctions which allow one group to dominate or exclude another must be eliminated. Paul's point is that the unity of believers creates a single community in which differences like those between Jew and Greek, slave and free, male and female, and young and old are not as important as their unity in Christ. Baptism calls us to a community of mutual relationships where individuals know how to give to and receive from one another regardless of age differences. A statement by John R. Silber shortly after he was inaugurated president of Boston University relates Paul's formula directly to the question of young and old.

> If we reorder time to celebrate youth and age and the gradual metamorphosis from one to the other, if we regain our sense of time, and value the present differences in the recognition that each of us plays all the parts in the sequence, we shall see that there is no salvation for the young or old at the expense of either.[2]

When relationships between young and old are not truly mutual, both suffer.

In place of a one-sided emphasis on either dependence or independence, Paul presents the ideal of interdependence. This is the meaning of his famous metaphor of the Christian community as the body of Christ. In 1 Corinthians 12, Paul talks about the diversity of gifts in the Christian community. All gifts have their source in the one Spirit and contribute to building up the one body of Christ. Just as in the human body each part or member contributes to an organic whole, so with the gifts of Christians. The body cannot be identified with any of its many parts, nor can any of the parts take the place of any other. Each contributes to the whole, and the whole depends on the proper functioning of every part. Mark Van Doren captures Paul's idea in his poem "All Seasons." He writes: "All seasons beautify the world and bless the walkers on it."[3]

The metaphor of the body is sometimes used to convey an organic view of human life. Such an understanding of life is basic to the contemporary movement called process philosophy. In this view of the world, dependence is an intrinsic dimension of all existence. Interdependence is a fact of life and does not decrease personal worth. We begin our life as a gift from others and The Other, God. Life is lived in communion from the beginning. Our existence is always partly a gift from others; we feed upon one another. Farmers produce the food we eat; artists, writers, and philosophers contribute to the growth of our minds and spirits. We turn to friends for courage and support; all those people we come into contact with enter in some way into the fabric of our being. Maturity is not defined exclusively in terms of independence; rather, it is the ability both to give and to receive, to influence and to be influenced.

According to process thought, we are all involved in mutually creative relationships, and these relations are internal, not simply external. That is, they are not simply accidental additions to our lives, like the wardrobe we change with the seasons. Insofar as we influence one another, we assimilate one another. As John Donne reminds us, "No man is an island," and every person's death diminishes each of us. Others are really present in our process of becoming.

Paul's metaphor of the body also reminds us that dependence and independence have many dimensions. It is a great illusion to believe that there are two kinds of human beings, the strong and the weak. Rather, we are all strong and weak in different ways. Instead of seeing mental and physical impairments as signs of incompetence, we need to look at them in terms of degrees of capacity and limitation. Physical frailty does not necessarily mean that we are incapable of making decisions. We may need help getting from place to place, but know more than we have ever known about making good choices. This multi-dimensionality of dependence and independence is beautifully portrayed in Joseph Lash's biography of Helen Keller, *Helen and Teacher*.[4] Although totally dependent on her teacher Anne Sullivan Macy for the most elemental tools of human communication and learning, for language itself, Helen Keller nonetheless was a remarkably independent woman. She held her own convictions in both the religious and political spheres, becoming a Swedenborgian at age sixteen and later also an ardent suffragist and radical socialist, much to her teacher's chagrin. Helen Keller's life shows us well that recognition of dependence, even deep and extensive dependence on another, need not mean loss of personal originality, autonomy, and influence. In the life of Jesus we see this same linkage of personal freedom and originality with strong dependence. Jesus depended on God for his life and direction; he needed the support of his disciples, especially in the Garden of Gethsemane. Yet he also remained a free person, choosing the course of his life up to the end.

## Receiving as a Way of Loving

Love takes on new meaning in a community built on mutuality. I learned this in the spring of 1981 when I led a poetry discussion group for a dozen residents of a nursing home. Many of the participants were in wheelchairs. Several were hard of hearing or nearly deaf. Two had very limited eyesight. One could not speak clearly enough to participate verbally in the group; another could not hold a piece of paper. One was in intense pain from the final stages of cancer. To the casual observer they probably appeared to be a very frail group of elderly.

Yet they had learned the meaning of Paul's image of the body; they knew that gifts are given for the building up of the whole. They also knew how to balance dependence and independence. Members who could see, read out loud so that those with limited sight could hear the lines. Those with hearing difficulties followed the printed poems. Ambulatory residents wheeled in those in wheelchairs, and those with steady hands secured papers for members who had difficulty holding them. Those who could not speak listened, laughed, and applauded the contributions of others. Together they discovered new beauty in the poems and in their own lives.

I was enriched most of all. For the last session I wrote a poem to thank them for all I had received during our Thursday mornings together. As I finished reading it, one of the women in her nineties said to me: "I cannot tell you what it means to hear you say that we have *given* you something. Most people think we are in here because we are useless."

All of us need assurance that we are loved. Our identity and security depend on the confirmation that we are accepted by others. The Christian community is meant to be a place where we find such assurance. But we have been brought up to think that love means giving. We love people by helping them, by doing things for them. That is, of course, one aspect of it. But it is only part of the exchange of love. Older persons often feel unloved, not because no one is willing to do things for them, but because people no longer value and receive their gifts. They do not want to be objects of pity or duty; they want human recognition, welcome, and a sense of belonging. They want more than sympathy and kindness; they want to be able to give as well as to receive, to be recognized as persons who have something to contribute. Many religious groups still speak of ministry *to* the elderly, without also thinking in terms of the ministries *of* and *by* the elderly. Only gradually are we recognizing that one of the best ways to love any member of the Christian community is to receive that person's gifts. A sense of usefulness to a community does not come from "busywork" or hobbies; there must be real give-and-take with others. This is especially true of the older members of that community. We need to call forth their gifts as spiritual directors, grief counselors, liturgical leaders, and teachers. Not only are their gifts ready at hand to be recognized, but the experience of being loved will free them to develop others.

This mutual exchange of gifts is exemplified in the networks of widows which developed during the first Christian centuries. Early Christian tradition reveals that widows were not only the object of charity; they formed one of the earliest societies of women in the Church. Widows filled certain needs of the Christian community and in turn were supported by it (Acts 6:1–3; 9:36–42). 1 Timothy 5:9–10 tells us that women had to be at least sixty years old to belong to this network of widows. Some of their contributions to the Christian community included teaching women prisoners, visiting sick women, providing encouragement and leadership in prayer, and anointing the dying, both men and women. In contrast, Helen Lopata says in her study of contemporary American widows that one of their problems is that they receive too much of the wrong kind of advice, when what they really need is help with grief work, companionship, the building of competence and self-confidence, and help in re-engagement.[5]

One of the most important contributions older persons make to a Christian community is the sharing of their stories of faith. As bearers of living tradition, they know stages of the Christian journey not yet experienced by the young. A ninety-four year old man, sitting on his porch step one evening, put it this way: "As we live more and study more and hear more, it gets deeper. And you don't know what to think until the end and it gets deeper yet." When I asked a group of students what gifts they had received from the older adults in their Christian communities, their responses emphasized these faith stories. One man in his thirties said that what impressed him the most was *how long* these older people had continued to believe, and the courage that had sometimes required. Another young woman shared the following reflection:

One thing these older people have taught me is an appreciation for people's stories. We all have a story to tell, no matter how old or young, no matter how literate or illiterate we are. It is amazing to me, too, to see how willingly most seniors share deeply of themselves—of their struggles, their joys, their family, their heritage, their faith and values. It is almost as if, reaching a certain age, the universality of our human experience is made clear and there is an urgency to share what has been learned—either easily or with much suffering—if it will make the way easier for an emerging adult like myself.

The sharing of stories can unify persons across generations, whereas discussing ideas sometimes isolates and divides. In stories we discover our common faith journey.

Some older people think that their stories must be edifying or reflect wonderful deeds if they are to be useful to the young. But sometimes younger persons simply want to know first-hand about the Church of a previous period. We learn by contrast, and many persons attempting to understand, for example, the post-Vatican II Church want to know what it was like before the Council met. The stories of older persons fill in details they have never known. I also remember a young high school student who told me how much he wanted to get to know his own grandmother. However, each time she began to tell him her life story, she would break off and say, "You wouldn't be interested in knowing that. You have more important things to think about." He was too shy to tell her how much he really did want to hear that story. Consequently, both lost a wonderful opportunity to know each other better.

Actually it is often stories of doubt and hard-won courage that sustain the young in their faith journey. One older man told a group about his lifelong struggle with the problem of evil. When he was growing up, he recalled, he had studied the Bible and found it easy to believe. Then, just as he finished high school, World War I broke out. He was sent to fight with the army on the front, and for the first time in his life he saw men kill one another. It shocked and sickened him. One night as he lay on a bale of hay, looking up from the trenches at the bright moon in a clear sky, he reflected: "I am not yet a father. But if I were a father and saw my children killing one another, would I stand by without stopping them?" No, he thought. No, I could not do that. Since that day, he said, he has never ceased agonizing over the question of God's relationship to suffering and evil. People of many ages in the group recognized in his story their own similar questions. He, in turn, realized that he was not alone; there were other believers in the world like him.

This realization that the story of any one of us is somehow the story of us all came to me when I was a young woman looking through a photo album with my grandmother. We often spent time paging through this old album while she told me the story behind this or that picture. My grandmother had an effective way of assuring that I would really listen to her stories. If she noticed that my attention was lagging, she would simply shout, "Hey!" and I would be startled back to alertness. One night she paused over an apparently insignificant photo. In it my grandmother is sitting next to the driver's seat in their Model T Ford, staring out the front window. The car is parked on a large bridge, and my grandmother looks embarrassed and uncomfortable. She explained to me that the picture was taken as she first arrived in Oregon. My grandmother and grandfather had lost their farm in the Dakotas during the Depression of 1929, and had brought their family to the West, to start over again. In the car she struggled to find the courage to get out and stand on the bridge. She had never before stood on a bridge like that over water. "I can do the big things," she said. "I don't know why it's so hard to get up the courage to do the little things." As I looked at the picture and listened to her experience, I saw that my grandmother's story was also my story. Like her, I had trouble with the small acts of courage. We shared the same struggle.

The old are also enriched by the young. One older man said of the young people in his community: "It is wonderful to hear their laughter and to find out the latest changes in attitudes." Another man added: "I like their positive attitude, their sense of the possible." This mutual exchange of gifts is evident in many of the intergenerational programs now in existence, such as the Foster Grandparent Program, which enables persons age sixty and over to volunteer their services to help children with special needs. The youngsters in the program receive much needed love and kindness. They also get a new image of aging, and find that there is dignity, vitality, and experience in older adults. The elderly find greater self-esteem and confidence in being able to give love and share their years of experience. Such relationships often develop into friendships that are not based on age as a criterion, and therefore move across the generations. These ageless friendships provide mentors for the young and help cushion the blow of loss when death begins to take friends from an older person's own age group.

## Baptism into Jesus' Death and Resurrection

Paul knows that the mutual community he holds before Christians as an ideal will not come into being easily. That is why he reminds us that baptism has inserted us into the mystery of Jesus' dying and rising. If young and old are to become an interdependent community, each will have to let go and die in some ways in order that the new community may come to life. Nigel Noble's 1981 award-winning documentary film "Close Harmony" chronicles some aspects of this process. The film tells the story of a teacher at the Friends School in Brooklyn, New York, who brings her fourth and fifth graders together with a local group of senior adults to form an intergenerational chorus. A number of warm personal relationships develop between members of the two groups. But each has to let go of some ideas and practices so that this can happen. The young people are afraid that the senior adults won't like children, or won't answer the letters they write them. Some of the adults are also fearful that they will not be accepted. Both groups find that in order to have one musical production they will have to make adjustments. The children must slow down, and the adults must speed up so that they can walk hand in hand. When they do, they produce a poignant concert.

Such dying in order to give life to new forms of community is not restricted to intergenerational groups, though we are focusing on those here. In her book *The Unexpected Community*,[6] Arlie R. Hochschild describes the community created by forty widows living in a low-cost housing project, many at the poverty level. These women created a genuine community, a kind of extended family, in their housing unit. They watched over one another, shared one another's griefs and joys, and planned projects in the house and excursions together. They could have relaxed, Hochschild says, and considered their social debts paid. Instead they shared berry jam and homemade Swedish rolls, posted photographs of pink-cheeked grandchildren and relatives from "back East" for others to see, and reached out of their isolation into one another's lives.

What things might die if we reached across the generations to form one community? Both old and young would need to remember that we can open our hearts only to those who listen in order to understand us, not to those who seem ready to judge or direct us. Older adults could relinquish the urge to tell their middle-aged children how to live their lives, practicing patience and tolerance when the young seem unable to hear their warnings and repeat the same mistakes they themselves made. They might forego the desire to give advice or to insist that the way they did things in the past was the best way. Joining groups with a mixture of ages also means letting go of some fears. Sometimes older people think that the young do not like them or will not find them interesting; older people should expect to be accepted. Sometimes as we age we need to let our fear and resentment and even envy of the young die, so that we can learn from them as we hope they will learn from us. One attitude that isolates the old from the young is the notion that younger people have had too little experience to understand anything about life. As one older woman said to me, "You are too young to have ever suffered. You cannot possibly understand what I am talking about." I felt insulted. She was presuming to know a lot about me. Old people as well as young need to acknowledge the commonality of our experience.

Younger people must also exercise a kind of dying. They may need to relinquish some of their preoccupation with speed and efficiency, or learn to listen well to the same story told more than once, since telling it several times may be the way an older person integrates its meaning into his or her life. Younger and middle-aged persons may need to adjust their pace in conversation, on buses, streets, and in supermarkets and department stores. A friend told me of a clerk in a department store who stared disgustedly at the ceiling while an older woman in front of her searched through her purse for the correct change. It is just such small gestures that rob persons of their dignity and their will to be independent.

Above all, the young and middle-aged will need to let go of condescending attitudes. Older people hate the assumption that they no longer know anything, and cannot handle their lives. Once when I had finished a year of counseling sessions with an eighty-one year old woman, she searched for something to say to thank me. Finally she said, "You never patronized me," and she told me that was in her estimation the best compliment she could give me. One form of condescension is to try to protect older people from reality by not dealing honestly with them and telling them the truth. This is another way of saying that we no longer expect any real exchange from them. A woman in a nursing home met me in the hallway one day, very upset: "Why didn't my family tell me that my dear friend Laura's home was broken into last week? They said they didn't want to worry me. But now I worry all the more, wondering what else they aren't telling me."

The short story "Games" describes how such pretense affects a relationship. In the story, an old woman named Eleanor Vernor is becoming increasingly forgetful, and her neighbors worry about her living alone. Her daughter Laura, and Laura's husband Peter, decide that she should come to live with them. After the move takes place, Eleanor reflects on that first evening in their home.

> The evening I got here—I remember I was wearing a gray suit that I had decided to give to the Salvation Army but that Laura had laid out for me to wear on our trip—I was ill at ease. I stood in their strange kitchen and wondered whether I should sit or offer to make dinner or go to my room.
>
> There had been a haste about our departure, and now there was shame in the air. Laura and Peter put on their serious expressions and began again telling me how fond they were of me. I remember wishing they had told me instead that they could imagine how it is to have to give up dreaming and the possibility of justification that the future allows, to have to tolerate a mind that on occasion cannot follow the slight movements of the present moment, and, finally, to have to give up authority and independence. But I said nothing. Later on,

we talked again. "Do whatever you like, as you like it," they told me. "Keep your own hours. Go shopping, have friends in." Then they sent me to bed. And I said a pleasant "good night" as I went. I was caught in the trap of the games already.[7]

Often difficulties arise not between the very old and the very young, but between older persons and their middle-aged children. What most older parents really want is continued contact with their children along with continued independence. Often they do not need help except in time of illness. When help is needed, however, it is important to recall that in a mutual relationship decisions are not made *for* others. Rather, they emerge from within the relationship. This means that we do not decide what is best for older persons and then carry out the decision; the older person is involved as fully as possible every step of the way.

One way to enhance the freedom of all those involved in such a relationship is to explore as many options as possible. Perhaps an older person is becoming frail and the adult child worries about his or her living alone. Some children simply decide what is best for their parents and carry out the decision, at times without even consulting the older person. However when the decision is made from within the relationship, it is clear that what is right for one older person and his or her family may be wrong for another. Two examples may help to clarify this.[8] Helen's parents are in their early eighties and her father is becoming very forgetful. Her mother is trying to care for him in spite of her own failing health. Helen lives alone now that her two children are away at college, and she gets along well with her parents. When Helen and her parents come together to discuss the decision, they decide that it would work out well for all of them if they came to live with her.

On the other hand, when Bob talks to his recently widowed sixty year old mother about coming to live with him, they determine together that it would not be a good idea. Bob worries about his mother since his father died, but she is in another part of the country and too far away for him to check on her easily. He and his wife think it would be great if his mother joined them in the small farming community where they live. What his mother tells them, however, is that she is well and happy where she is. She is used to a lively social life with lifelong friends in New York, and has some jury duty and part-time work to keep her busy. She would be bored and lonely in their farming community. Such decisions are not without conflict and pain, but when they are made in a mutual way, all learn more about one another and grow in the process. It should be added, that we do not lose the right to make mistakes and to fail when we age; these are part of freedom at any point in the life cycle.

In reflecting on the relationship between older persons and their adult children, it is helpful to remember that we do not enter into a "second childhood" when we grow old. The dependencies of later life are not the same as those of early childhood, and the relationship between adult children and their parents is not one of reversal of roles. A term that has been coined to describe the role of an adult son or daughter in relation to an aging parent is "filial maturity."[9] There is a point in the life cycle when being a son or daughter means seeing one's parents now as a mature adult sees them, that is, as persons with their own strengths and weaknesses, needs and rights, and individual life histories. Being a son or daughter at this stage demands a certain freedom from one's parents and the resolution of unresolved rebellion which may have begun in adolescence. It is also a readiness to provide assistance in times of stress or trouble.

The interdependent community Paul describes is centered in the crucified and risen Jesus. Mutual relationships are difficult to carry out and, as was the case with Jesus, they involve us in the cross and suffering. There will always be conflicts between generations, but such conflict can be used creatively as a way to human growth and change. When young, middle-aged, and older persons are actively open to one another, they will encounter the contrasts that are part of these different points in the life cycle. Such contrasts provide challenge, but challenge is as important to health and happiness as comfort. Relationships involving contrasts also increase the beauty of all involved, for greater contrast intensifies the beauty of the whole. A hillside that is entirely green is not nearly as lovely as one with bright colorful flowers sharply etched against the green. Add a deep blue sky and floating white clouds, and you have still another dimension of beauty. So, too, the Christian community is enriched when young and old come together to share their gifts.

# 5

# **LOVE AND SEXUALITY**

During a single lifetime we know love in many forms. As small children we experience the love of our parents and grandparents, of favorite pets, and of first friends. Later we realize the excitement of falling in love, the heartache that accompanies the loss of a love, the joys of faithful relationships. But there are dimensions of love which can only be experienced in the later years. The poet Archibald MacLeish says,

> Ours is the late, last wisdom of the afternoon.
> We know that love, like light, grows dearer toward
> the dark.[1]

Only then has there been time enough fully to discover ourselves and others in relationship, and to know those qualities of friendship which emerge with the passage of years. In Edwin Arlington Robinson's poem, "Isaac and Archibald," Isaac speaks to a twelve year old boy of his old friend Archibald.

> But I have known him in and out so long,
> And I have seen so much of good in him
> That other men have shared and have not seen,
> And I have gone so far through thick and thin,

Through cold and fire with him, that now it brings
To this old heart of mine an ache that you
Have not yet lived enough to know about.[2]

Jesus tells us that the meaning of human life is found in communion with others. In this light we can see the whole course of our life as a journey into the heart of love. The story of Jane, a friend of mine, illustrates this truth. Jane's mother died in a nursing home several years ago at the age of ninety. Jane and her mother were together often during her mother's last years, but they found that gradually there was less and less to say. Toward the end they simply stopped talking, comfortable with a shared silence. Attached to the dashboard in Jane's car was a heart-shaped magnet inscribed with the single word Love. Jane recalls how, during their final year together, her mother would often reach up and touch the heart, and then pat Jane's knee. All else was slipping away. Love alone remained.

Love not only opens us to the mystery of human life. It also reveals God to us. In 1 John 4:7–12, we are reminded that no one has ever seen God, but that everyone who loves knows God. Human love is a sacrament of God's love for us. It not only enables us to trust that God actually loves us; it embodies that love, making it visible and tangible in our lives. Through human friendship we learn the comfort, challenge, fidelity and healing of God. This happens in very simple ways. Friends help with shopping and cleaning during times of sickness. They get us out and active again after a loss. They send letters or telephone to share news and let us know they are thinking of us. They listen to all our joys and sorrows. They reach out to take our hand, offer us the warmth of touch, or hold us. Older people are frequently told that it does not matter if their productivity declines with age, since lasting self-worth is grounded in God's love. True as this is, it is difficult to experience it unless God's love is mediated to us through genuine human love in our lives.

Since love is the center of Christian discipleship, it is clear that Jesus' command to love others becomes more, not less, important as we age. It may also become more challenging. The loss of close friends, our winter companions, removes familiar circles of love. Society's devaluing of us erodes our confidence that we have gifts to offer others. Physical limitations and illness can turn our attention inward until we become preoccupied with our own aches and pains. A ninety-six year old man once told me that he did not like to be around older people. "They've let their hearts shrivel up," he said. "All they can talk about is the present state of their own health." Certainly, that need not happen. Francois Mauriac reflects on this same question.

> One must hope to grow old keeping one's life and background richly filled, hope to live so that people need us and we need them until the end. Nothing, of course, can prevent old age from being a desert, an expanse of sand that gradually covers and smothers everything. But it is for us to preserve enough strength to plant and people our desert, to create oases in the midst of our solitude.[3]

The Gospel calls us not only to people this desert, but to deepen and expand the quality of our love in the later years. It also assures us that this is the way to real happiness.

Social scientists today are exploring more fully several aspects of love in later life. In this chapter we will look at the spiritual implications of their findings in three areas: (1) love and sex after sixty, (2) the importance of friendship in the later years, and (3) the call to compassion and universal love.

## Love and Sex after Sixty

We are at last beginning to challenge the stereotypes surrounding sexuality and aging. During the past decade several films have dealt in new ways with the importance of love and sexuality in later life: "On Golden Pond," "Tell Me a Riddle," "Harold and Maude." In 1982 Bette Davis starred in the critically acclaimed "A Piano for Mrs. Cimino," the story of a seventy-three year old widow's struggles to resist the stigmas that society places on the elderly. There are hopeful signs that we are beginning to recognize the dimensions of human sexuality that mature in the later years.

Sexuality is the basis for entering into relationships that enhance our lives. It is an enduring dimension of the human personality, and contributes energy and warmth to all of the ways we relate with others. Our sexuality is broader than sex or genital activity; it is a power of attraction, communication and compassion in human life. Sexuality is dynamic and so it has many stages and many meanings.

In the past we assumed that older persons had little interest in their sexuality and no longer actively engaged in sex. The sources of such stereotyping are complex: adult children's difficulty in recognizing their parents as sexual beings, inaccurate information concerning the physical aspects of aging, and societal prejudices that reserved sex for the young and vigorous and portrayed the old as withered and infirm. Religion contributed to this stereotyping by linking sex so exclusively with child-bearing that it seemed to lose its reason for existing after the parenting years were past. However, many couples now live two or three decades beyond the years when sexuality is linked with reproduction. Concepts other than motherhood and fatherhood will be important in shaping images of femininity and masculinity during these years.

Recent writing has done much to illumine this misunderstood aspect of later life.[4] While our sexual capacity, like other functioning, declines somewhat with age, sexual activity can and does continue into advanced age, the eighties and beyond. In some cases sexual interest and activity increase over the years. Age, in any case, is not the decisive determinant. A number of physical, psychological and social factors influence our sexual lives as we age. Poverty, lack of privacy, depression, nutrition, and society's attitudes strongly affect the sexual activity of older men and women.

Helpful and necessary as this recent research has been, it has focused mainly on the physical aspects of sex. In an effort to counteract current misconceptions it has emphasized the elderly's continued capacity for sexual performance. While it is important to point out that the physiological changes connected with aging do not dramatically affect the capacity for sexual arousal, intercourse, and orgasm, it is a mistake to use these as the major norm for evaluating sexuality in later life. There is danger that youth will once again be the standard by which the later years are judged. Perhaps it is time to reverse this one-sided standard and allow older people to share important insights which can help all ages better understand the meaning of human sex and sexuality.

Older people are better able to understand sex as a deep form of communication, and to recognize its relational dimensions. They have lived a long time, and have had years of experience in giving and receiving. Many elderly have developed more fully the place of affection in their relationship, and have learned to enjoy touching, lying together, and holding one another in slower paced and less performance oriented love making. They are able to realize more clearly that expressions of love must exist within the context of a loving relationship. One older woman described the relationships of older couples in this way:

> In many long-term marriage relationships there develops an almost overpowering bond of concern and empathy, a desire to nurture and defend, a fierce joy in the other's growth and success, and a deeply felt tenderness and love that sees the beauty and worth of the beloved beyond any signs of aging or disability. The expression of these loving emotions may be in part sexual, but these feelings, which are the essence of friendship and total acceptance of another, transcend the genital act.

In *Love and Sex after Sixty,* Butler and Lewis refer to that sexual expression which is emotional and communicative as well as physical as the second language of sex. They find that older people have a number of qualities which beautifully prepare them to speak this second language, including their struggle to come to terms with life as a cycle from birth to death, and their appreciation of the preciousness of life and of immediacy.[5] Many people are too preoccupied with results to experience the joy that can come from this deeper process of communication and caring.

Older men and women continue to be revelation and grace for each other and for the Christian community. In the way they love, each reveals God to the other, for God is love. Certain aspects of this love of God can best be made visibly and tangibly present in long-standing relationships: God's faithfulness and forgiveness of repeated failures, a divine love that knows us intimately, and love as companionship and compassion in the midst of suffering. Such a love integrates sorrow and pain.

> Love, as the old know love.
> Fibred with grief, it is strong.[6]

Other Christians need the insights into God's covenant which the relationships of older couples provide. A young woman in her late twenties said that as she struggled with the choice of a permanent commitment in marriage, she learned something of its meaning from a man married for many years.

> An elderly man who had taken care of his wife's most basic needs for the past seven years, after she had suffered a series of strokes that left her severely brain damaged, taught me much about love and fidelity. His wife certainly was not the healthy young person he had been "in love" with during their early years. And yet the words "till death do us part" were taken very seriously by him.

Older couples reveal to all of us some of the most important qualities for the journey of love.

In turn, older persons need the support of the Christian community in meeting the challenges peculiar to the last stages of loving. Older persons have discovered the limitations and frustrations, the pain and ambiguities of human love. If years of relating can deepen understanding and communion, they can also solidify misunderstanding and alienation. An older couple may find that their love has deteriorated, that they are still harboring past hurts, or that their partner has changed during the years and they are now relating to a different person. Older couples are together more hours each day than in previous years, and this can also accentuate problems. The gifted fiction writer Tillie Olsen opens her novella *Tell Me a Riddle* with a description of such an experience.

> For forty-seven years they had been married. How deep back the stubborn, gnarled roots of the quarrel reached, no one could say—but only now, when tending to the needs of others no longer shackled them together, the roots swelled up visible, split the earth between them, and the tearing shook even to the children, long since grown.[7]

The stresses of the later years, such as retirement and ill health, can revive long-standing problems or place unexpected strains on an otherwise healthy relationship. A vigorous and healthy man in his late sixties experienced such stress when his wife suddenly needed nursing home placement. Her decline had been rapid, complicated by a fall in their home, and he found himself no longer able to care for her. Before her illness they had purchased a large van and made plans to travel and explore the outdoors, something they both enjoyed. Now he saw his hopes for retirement evaporate. He struggled with that reality, and then saw what he needed to do. He equipped the van instead with a wheel chair lift for transporting his wife to doctor's appointments and on brief outings. "I felt myself called," he said, "to a level of fidelity I had never experienced before." Older couples need the support and resources of the Christian community in working through the challenges of love in their last decades.

Remarriage is also an important question for the Christian community. The number of older persons choosing to marry again after the loss of a spouse has increased and will continue to grow. And why shouldn't it? The greatest opposition to such marriages frequently comes from adult children who may feel guilt about their own inability to care for their widowed parent, who think of marriage as reserved for young people, or who are afraid of losing an inheritance. Approval of such marriages by children and friends is, however, vital to their success. The Christian community needs to find ways to celebrate and affirm them.

## The Importance of Friendship in the Later Years

Many older persons have told me that next to good health, the most important ingredient of happiness in later life is "not to be alone." To the end of our lives we need the closeness to others which we call intimacy; in fact, the need for intimacy may be heightened in the later years because of multiple losses. There is a temptation to give up on the Christian command to love others as we grow old because we may be afraid to talk to one another or to touch one another. It is sometimes difficult to initiate personal relationships or to participate in situations that require sharing. Above all, it is hard to find new sources of intimacy to replace those taken from us as we age.

Intimacy develops in romantic friendships and sexual relationships, but it is also found in many different kinds of friendships and in cooperating with others on common concerns and projects. While the degree and shape of intimacy varies, every friendship is in some way an intimate relationship. For friendship is one of the ways in which we come close to another, whether this friend be a spouse, a neighbor, a lifelong confidant, or a recent companion discovered through the pursuit of a new interest. Intimacy has many dimensions, including mutual support and understanding, trust and the sharing of confidences. Through intimate relationships we enter into another's life, and receive the gift of their life in return.

Studies show that the existence of an intimate other is very important to satisfaction and psychological well-being in later life.[8] Such intimacy helps prevent depression and anxiety. It gives security and significance to life. In the words of some older people themselves, it is "a port in the storm," and "the ultimate closeness against the night."[9] One woman told me that her friend across the street "made all the difference" in her ability to cope with life.

In view of the critical importance of an intimate relationship up to the very end of life, some researchers have wondered whether woman's greater openness to close relationships accounts for her greater ability to survive. Not only is the overall death rate higher among men, but with age the suicide rate increases rapidly among men but not among women. And although men have more opportunities for remarriage than women, widowhood triggers more mental illness among men than among women. Perhaps because society discourages men from the development of kinds of intimacy other than the purely sexual, they have fewer alternatives than women for intimate relationships in advanced age.[10]

Friendship is religiously important as well. One of the things we find most difficult to believe over the course of a lifetime is that we are worthwhile enough to be loved by God. The discovery that we are important to and loved by other human beings makes this truth credible. From our experience of loving concern and compassion in human relationships we learn that God is caring and compassionate. Friendships also help us to grow in faith during periods of crisis. When our faith is challenged by suffering and disappointments, and by the inevitability of death, the witness and assistance of a friend's faith can deepen our own.[11]

Although the later years bring the loss of some friendships, they can also be a time of special opportunities for nourishing relationships. Throughout their lives many people affirm the truism that it is relationships which give meaning to life. Philosophers and theologians support this common conviction with elaborate theories and arguments. In actual practice, however, many individuals devote much of their time and energy to other aspects of their lives: going to school and getting a degree, beginning and developing a career, establishing and paying for a home, making money and laying a secure financial foundation for the future. In short, though we affirm the centrality of relationships, we live in terms of the values of productivity and consumerism.

Older persons have the opportunity to actually live the value of friendship and to sacramentalize its importance for others. They, perhaps more than any other age group, can really put relationships first in their lives. When he was interviewed after his retirement as editor of *The Nation,* the writer Carey McWilliams commented:

> . . . . from 1951 until the time I resigned I lived such a rat-race existence, night and day, weekend, vacation time, whatnot—no staff, you know? Incredible rat race. Then when I retired, I suddenly began to see human relations and personal relations in terms that I hadn't been aware of. Been too busy, really, to perceive. Well, I found out a lot of interesting things. Nuances about relations between people. I had more time to listen to

them. More time to perceive. More time to spend
with my wife. More time to become aware of her
problems, problems of being a wife with intellec-
tual interests of her own. . . . I got a much better
feel for personal relations just simply because I've
had some time to observe and to meditate a bit
about it, think about it.[12]

The later years can be a time for living out the values we
affirm much of our life, by attending to the details of love.

A dimension of human relating particularly important
to later life is touch. Christian faith takes embodiment seri-
ously, for we believe that the "the Word became flesh" (Jn
1:14), and continues to become flesh through our love of
others. Our bodies express who we are; through our gestures, expressions, and postures, we articulate the language
of the self. Alfred North Whitehead speaks of the human
body as the primary field of human expression. Older people can easily feel alienated from their bodies. Once when
I took the hand of a woman in her sixties, she said to me,
"You know, it has been nearly three years since anyone
touched me in a loving way." Another woman told me that
it felt so good to be held by someone, but that it rarely happened to her. It is harder to affirm a bodily self that is limited, painful, and declining. Some, like those who experience the crippling effects of a stroke, feel angry at their
bodies and fear further alterations or becoming ill and help-
less. The loving touch of others heals and affirms us in a
total way. We need to be touched in order to believe that
we are alive and matter to others. Human touch also
reveals to us, especially as we age, the mystery found in an
embodied and hidden Jesus: it is in the weakness of human
flesh that God is revealed. There is spiritual power hidden
in human vulnerability.[13]

## The Call to Compassion and Universal Love

Maggie Kuhn, the seventy-eight year old founder of the Gray Panthers, speaks of older persons as the tribal elders. And, she says, the tribal elders are concerned about the tribe's survival. The Gray Panthers, which she founded as an advocacy group for the elderly on social issues, has made peace one of its top two priorities. As this action indicates, the later years offer us the possibility of a growing sense of communion with all beings. Our capacity to love becomes a celebration of life and a desire to see that it is preserved for succeeding generations. We are aware that we belong to a community across time; we are therefore willing to labor to build bridges that we will never cross because we know that others, younger than we, will someday need them. In his poem "Hardy Perennial," Richard Eberhart says,

> I would give love to every being alive,
> Penetrating the secrets of the living.[14]

As we age, our love can become more universal and compassionate. Compassion is the ability to hear the expression of another's concern and respond to it as our own. It is a crucial Christian virtue in a global community characterized as ours is by both interdependence and inequality. Because it enables us to embrace the concerns of others, compassion is a form of hope, hope for a future beyond self. As we age, the horizons of life can narrow. One of my favorite older friends is a ninety-four year old man who constantly tries to broaden the vision of all people, young and old. "We need to train our children, not with the idea of competition, but with the idea of service to others," he says. "I try to be kind and loving to people. If we were all that way, there wouldn't be any war." Aging can be a time of expanding horizons, like a river widening out to the larger sea.

The process of aging involves an inevitable self-emptying. But like Jesus' self-emptying, it can become a way of identifying with humanity in order to liberate it from suffering. Jesus accepts our humanity and joins our experience of broken dreams and lost hopes. In this way he accomplishes the divine work of reconciliation.

> His state was divine
> yet he did not cling
> to his equality with God
> but emptied himself . . .
> and became as humans are (Phil 2:6–7).

Like the servant of Isaiah 13, Jesus gives his life for the many.

Love in the later years is like the self-emptying love of Jesus. By that point in our journey we have entered into the human situation much more deeply than at earlier stages. Aging in itself involves a certain renunciation and detachment, a purification of self-interest. Compassion is one way our sufferings borne over a lifetime can become sources of redemption for others. Because we have known suffering in ourselves, we are aware that others suffer too. That knowledge can enable us to enter into their lives. When I know what it is for others also to suffer, I am drawn to provide some relief, support and care for them in their suffering. May Sarton uses an apt image to describe this kind of love: "Odd, isn't it? How these quarries, blasted open by dynamite, the scene of so much violence, so much lifting and carrying too, after they are abandoned, become magic places, deep ponds."[15] The self-emptying that accompanies aging is not simply waste; it implies a mission to exist for others. If it follows the pattern of Jesus, it is at the service of love. Such a capacity to live for others and to give one's life on behalf of a shared humanity is one dimension of Christian courage.

It is this kind of love that motivates a group of senior adults in California. The group gathers surplus produce from California farms and distributes it to the sick, the elderly and the needy. In one year they saved over eight hundred tons of produce that would otherwise have been left to rot, been plowed under, or fed to hogs. They salvage produce such as potatoes that are perfectly edible but too gnarled to sell, tomatoes at the peak of their ripeness and so unsuited for long truck trips to the east coast market, and onions unacceptable solely because they are too large for hamburger buns. In so doing, they enlarge their love to include two national problems: hunger and waste.

Love in the later years need not be displayed on a dramatic scale. It can consist simply of a kind word or a visit to the lonely. Often it means listening to the sorrowing or the joyful, the old and the young, who need an attentive heart. In *The Desert Blooms,* Sarah-Patton Boyle describes the ministry of praise which she developed. She not only made it a point to offset some of the world's criticism by praising the gifts of those she knew, but she let strangers she dealt with, the bus driver, the grocery clerk, and their supervisors, know that she appreciated a job well done.[16] Dorothy Day often said that the only way she had of knowing and believing in her love of God was her love for ordinary people. She persevered in this love until the end, even when the forces of evil seemed overwhelming. She based her love on the hope that "bitter as it is today with ice and sleet, the sap will soon be rising in those bare trees down the street from us."[17]

# 6

# OLDER WOMEN

Not only is our population aging, but a majority of the elderly are women. Women have a longer life expectancy than men, and older women are the fastest-growing segment of our society. In 1900 there were actually fewer women than men over sixty-five, but by 1974 this relationship had changed so that there were 143 women per 100 men. If projections of population trends for the year 2000 prove true, women over sixty-five will constitute seven percent of the total population, outnumbering older men by a margin of 154 to 100.[1]

Growing old can be especially difficult for a woman. Older women are more likely than men to be poor and to be widowed. The average age of widowhood is fifty-six, and one-third of all widows live below the poverty line.[2] Poor health is also often a problem. While older men die sooner, older women have more illnesses. But what is perhaps most difficult of all for a woman as she ages is that she is burdened by more negative stereotypes than any other age group. She is neither young nor male. Men who age are said to reach greater maturity; women lose their youth. Susan Sontag refers to this as the double standard of aging.[3] As a result of this double standard, many women have difficulty adjusting to the loss of beauty and youth as these are defined by our culture. An eight billion dollar a year cosmetics industry keeps alive the notion that young is beautiful and old is ugly. As a result, body image and appearance anxiety are a major problem for many older women. Moreover, low self-image arises from the feeling that one is no longer needed and is subject to discard. This sense of worthlessness can lead to depression and patterns of self-neglect, or to alcoholism and drug abuse.

Spiritual growth for women in the later years means refusing to accept this equation of beauty with youth. When Lillian Oppenhiemer, known for her writing and teaching on origami, the art of Japanese paper folding, was approaching her eighties, a friend wrote to her: "You are like the flowers, lovelier now than in your distant spring."[4] Older women must begin to believe in the beauty found in their mature lives, and in turn offer new images of aging to society. Younger and middle-aged women are searching for viable models of older women to follow. A Peanuts cartoon strip states this in a delightful way. Lucy, reading a composition to her class, says:

And so World War II came to an end. My grandmother left her job in the defense plant and went to work for the telephone company. We need to study the lives of great women like my grandmother. Talk to your own grandmother today. Ask her questions. You'll find she knows more than peanut butter cookies! Thank you!

The survival of humanity itself depends on utilizing fully the energy of mature women. Older women are a resource which a society faced with possible ecological disaster or nuclear holocaust can no longer afford to neglect.

Countering society's image of older women is not an easy task. What spiritual resources can women draw on as they attempt it? This chapter will look to several biblical women for insights: Martha, Anna, two New Testament widows, Mary the Mother of Jesus, Naomi, and Elizabeth. These biblical women are as diverse as older women themselves, but together they illumine experiences which many older women face.

## Martha, Woman of Lively Faith

In the past we thought of Martha as busy and bustling in the kitchen while her sister Mary chose the better part, quiet contemplation at Jesus' feet. Recently, however, we have rediscovered strands of the Christian tradition which portray Martha as a woman of mature and lively faith. For a long time the tradition followed only Luke's story in 10:38–42, where Martha serves at table and Mary listens at Jesus' feet. About 1300, the Dominican mystic and monk, Meister Eckhart, in preaching on Luke's story of Mary and Martha, speaks of the active creativity of Martha, something the younger Mary would know only when she had learned to live. Eckhart pictures Martha as a woman concerned for her responsibilities and the world.

Although we are more familiar with the portrayal of Martha in Luke's Gospel, John provides a different portrait of her. In John 11:1–44 Martha has just lost her brother Lazarus. When Lazarus became ill, she and her sister Mary sent word to their friend Jesus. Martha cannot understand why Jesus waited so long to respond to their message. By the time Jesus finally arrives, Martha is in the midst of a house full of mourners. Her brother is dead. She goes out to meet Jesus with a greeting filled with grief and disappointment: "If you had been here, my brother would not have died." How could Jesus have failed her so?

Martha's conversation with Jesus reveals a woman of active faith. She believes that the resurrection will occur in the future, but she wants some help now. To Jesus' statement, "Your brother will rise again," Martha responds, "I know he will rise again at the resurrection on the last day." Like Job, Martha struggles with the mystery of suffering and the ways of God. The reality of future resurrection does not erase the pain of present losses. Martha's questioning is evidence of the seriousness of her faith, and during her discussion with Jesus she receives a major revelation of his identity: "I am the resurrection." She, in turn, recognizes him as Messiah: "Yes, Lord," she said. "I believe that you are the Christ, the Son of God, the one who was to come into the world."

Many older women share Martha's passionate, questioning faith. A woman in her seventies whose two sons had both died within a year of each other said to me one day: "I lost my boys. I search in prayer for a way through this loss. I need them with me here, not just in the hereafter." Another woman in her eighties wrestles with the faith question of the survivor. One day, after we had been talking for some months about her bouts with depression, she said to me: "Do you know what I really want to know? I want to know why God lets me live. My daughter died last year when her family needed her. My sister died several years ago, even though there were people who still depended on her. No one needs me. So why does God let me live?" As with Martha, the questioning does not negate the faith of these older women. They continue to believe and to trust—but also to struggle. Their questioning is a part of the maturity and liveliness of their faith.

In *The Women Around Jesus,* Elisabeth Moltmann-Wendel uncovers other insights into Martha by examining the art of the fourteenth and fifteenth centuries. In this art

Martha is no longer simply the woman who chooses action over contemplation. She attains a new sense of importance as an older woman: "Her beauty is the beauty of maturity."[5] Though overshadowed earlier by her more attractive sister Mary, during these centuries Martha moves to the forefront as a spiritual and competent woman. For example, a painting by the Dominican Fra Angelico depicts the scene of Jesus' prayer in Gethsemane. In the background Jesus prays that the cup of crucifixion may pass from him. At left of center, Peter, James and John are overcome by sleep. But to the right, in the foreground, Martha and Mary sit awake, keeping watch. Mary, with bowed head, reads a book. Martha is fully alert and prays with uplifted hands, adopting the same attitude as Jesus in the background. Elisabeth Moltmann-Wendel comments:

> Contemplation and action, the characteristics of the two sisters, are still recognizable. However, the action of Martha is now a readiness to watch with Jesus which has grown from her own total involvement, her own spirituality. The disciples are the ones who fail, who fall asleep.[6]

It is the women who see things through to the end. Martha perseveres in Gethsemane's dark hour of human failure.

Martha provides a strong image of an older woman of faith. Her faith is still alive and growing. She meets its challenges with both honesty and fidelity. Jesus responds to this faith with the revelation of himself, and she becomes one of the first to know that Jesus is himself the resurrection. Writing of the older woman in *Knowing Woman,* Irene Claremont de Castillejo says that the curve of woman's life span follows the pattern of the seasons. She blossoms in spring, and there is a long summer of very slow ripening.

But "the autumn of a woman's life is far richer than the spring if only she becomes aware in time, and harvests the ripening fruit before it falls and rots and is trampled under-foot. The winter which follows is not barren if the harvest has been stored, and the withdrawal of sap is only a prelude to a new spring elsewhere."[7] Martha reveals something of this kind of mature beauty.

### Anna: A Woman Awaiting the Future

Luke describes Anna as a prophetess, a descendant of the ancient tribe of Asher (Lk 2:36–38). She witnesses to God by the holiness of her life and by speaking in his name. The Gospel says that the days of her girlhood are gone, and gives her age as eighty-four. Anna is no longer young, but she is apparently not troubled by the fact.

In fact, the message Anna shares with others is one of hope and salvation: "She spoke of the child to all who looked forward to the deliverance of Jerusalem." Anna appears in the Gospel for only a brief moment, but reveals herself as a woman of prayer who longs for the salvation of her people and points them toward the true source of hap-piness. Luke emphasizes that her words are not intended simply for one age or race, but for all people. The words of a contemporary older woman expand our understanding of Anna's role. Maggie Kuhn, the leader of the Gray Panthers, believes that there must be something providential in the fact that there are so many older people today, close to twenty-three million sixty-five years and older: "It may be that God looked down upon our sick and ailing and divided world and said, 'Aha! I will raise some new revo-lutionaries to point the way.' It might be that those of us who are nearest death could be chosen by God to point to where new life can be found."[8] One way that many older women are pointing the way to life is through their concern for world peace. Two seventy-nine year old women recently demonstrated the active compassion that often accompanies the later years. Ruth Nelson is a former National Mother of the Year who in the summer of 1982 joined in protesting the arrival of the Trident submarine at Bangor, Washington. The mother of seven children, three of whom are adopted, she said in an interview after the protest, "I have always loved the whole person. Whether or not it means my life, I have to say 'no' to death and 'yes' to life." Part of what sustains her in her work for peace is the conviction that each of us can make a difference. She sees her role as that of a climate-changer, eliminating the dinosaurs of hatred and hostility.

Very like Ruth is Terri Mead, also seventy-nine, who works on behalf of peace and the poor on the streets of San Francisco. A motivating force for her also is the belief that "you can never be sure if one person can make a difference. You have to do what you can do and hope it makes a difference." When the *San Francisco Chronicle* ran a story about Terri's participation in a Holy Week blockade at the Lawrence Livermore weapons research and development laboratory, it described her as old and "frail." One of her friends responded, "Terri frail? That woman's made of steel."

The role of pointing the way to new life takes as many shapes as there are older women. One member of a religious congregation, who officially retired after thirty-eight years of teaching first and second grade, spends her time helping with education programs in her parish and visiting with older people in retirement centers. "I don't look back," she told me. "I look ahead. Everything I have done has prepared me for the next step in life. I believe most of my experience has led up to where I am now, and I really feel I am using more of my gifts than ever before." For some older women, pointing the way to life means a ministry of prayer, prayer that is a work of justice. Others find that they now have time for a ministry of communication, writing letters that influence human rights throughout the world, or political decisions at home. In whatever ways they choose, older women need, like Anna, to share their gifts with the world, pointing it toward a future of true happiness and salvation.

**Jesus and Persistent Widows**

Jesus shows special affection for widows, who are among the most poor and oppressed people of his day. After the loss of their husbands, widows had almost no means of livelihood or standing before the law, nor anyone to provide for them. In a story in Luke 18:1–8 about the need to persevere in prayer, "The Widow and the Unjust Judge," Jesus praises the determination of a widow before bureaucratic bungling. The widow in the story is up against the powerful but self-confessedly corrupt establishment. Her opponent is probably a property owner. "There was a judge in a certain town," the story begins, "who had neither fear of God nor respect for human beings." A widow in the same town comes to him again and again asking for justice. The judge holds out as long as he can, but finally he reasons, "Maybe I have neither fear of God nor respect for human beings, but since she keeps pestering me I must give this widow her just rights, or she will persist in coming and hassle me to death."

Many older women must learn both to request things for themselves and to deal with powerful bureaucracies. Often they have been schooled to care for others, but not to ask for what they need. A woman in her seventies told me how she recognized such a split in herself. She had been a successful legal secretary, but growing health problems had eaten up her savings, and a chronic leg condition was now plaguing her. Her afflictions involved her in a muddle of medicaid forms, well-meaning social workers, and sporadic food deliveries. Attempting to find her way through all of the confusion, she said: "All my life I have been so good at requesting things for others. Now I am struggling to learn to ask for things for myself."

Sometimes the persistence is on behalf of others rather than ourselves. During a recent urban political dispute, several older women described themselves to me as feeling much like the widow in Luke's story. There was a move afoot to turn three blocks of low-income housing into a convention center. The women were working to prevent a decision which would leave many elderly and urban poor homeless. Arriving at a council hearing on the matter, they were seated opposite a number of well-dressed business executives, most from luxury city hotels that stood to profit from the new center. "I could see them looking at us so condescendingly," one of the women said. "They probably thought we were little old ladies with no power or punch. We were so proud when our representatives presented our case eloquently." These women did not get the results that the woman in the Gospel story did. Plans for the convention center moved ahead in spite of their opposition. But their persistence did result in greater public awareness of the housing needs of the poor and elderly.

Another Gospel story of a widow makes clear the true criteria for beauty. It is the account of "The Widow's Mite" in Luke 21:1-4. This brief passage describes a poverty-stricken widow who gives two small coins as her offering to the temple treasury. The rich are also making their contributions, but Jesus focuses on her gift: "I tell you truly, this poor widow has put in more than any of them; for these have all contributed money they had over, but she, from the little she had, has put in all she had to live on." What counts in life, Jesus is saying, is not external wealth, power, beauty and strength. It is one's generosity in giving what one has. It is the inner spirit and integrity of a person's life.

## Mary and the Circles of Time

At the annunciation Mary is asked to plunge into an adventure filled with uncertainty. The descriptions of her in the New Testament show her standing at the end of one age and the beginning of another. We may be living in such a time ourselves. When the angel first appears to her in Luke 1:26–38 she is a young faithful daughter of Israel. Mary is the only adult from Luke's infancy narratives who reappears in the course of Jesus' ministry. A new age has begun by the time Acts 1:12–14 includes her among the first Christian disciples gathered in the upper room before Pentecost: "All these joined in continuous prayer, together with several women, including Mary the mother of Jesus." During her lifetime Mary must deal with all the changes involved in the dawning of that new age. She exhibits an amazing power of endurance.

By the time she appears in the upper room, Mary knows both the joys and the sorrows of motherhood. She does not always understand her son. When he is a child, Mary and Joseph take him to Jerusalem for the feast of Passover. Jesus remains behind in the temple when they return home, and Mary and Joseph search frantically for him. When they are reunited, Mary asks, "My child, why have you done this to us? See how worried your father and I have been, looking for you." Jesus replies that he has been about his Father's business, but "they did not understand what he meant" (Lk 2:41–52).

Luke does not leave Mary on the negative note of misunderstanding, however. He stresses that she retained what she had not yet understood, and continued to search for understanding: "His mother stored up all these things in her heart." This is the same way Luke depicts Mary's response to the joy and astonishment of the shepherds at the birth of Jesus: "As for Mary, she treasured all these things and pondered them in her heart" (2:19). Mary's prayerful gathering and sorting presents a model of contemplative motherhood. One day when we were speaking of Mary in a theology class, a woman who had been widowed for eight years remarked: "I look to her as a woman of quiet courage. I worry so about the problems of my children and grandchildren. My husband and I used to talk them over. Now I feel so alone with them. But Mary's years of trying to understand Jesus, and yet finding it hard, strengthen me in my own experience."

Mary appears only twice in John's Gospel. She is at the wedding in Cana where Jesus responds to her concern over the diminishing supply of wine by telling her that his "hour has not yet come" (Jn 2:5). When next we meet her, that hour is here. She is a widow standing at the foot of her son's cross. When the hour comes, she has a much richer role than before: "Seeing his mother and the disciple he loved standing near her, Jesus said to his mother, 'Woman, this is your son'" (Jn 19:26). Mary's motherhood is now a universal care for the world. She is still a mother, but a mother in an expanded sense that incorporates other aspects of her identity as well. Mary's motherhood is like a stone cast into a pond, producing concentric circles that grow ever wider. The outer circles owe their existence to the inner ones; the core is never abandoned.

Maturity, as Mary portrays it, is realized through a life of interdependence and care. She shows how women's integrity is entwined with concern for others, though the meaning and expression of this care may change over the course of a lifetime. Because woman's life is focused on caring, the loss of key relationships as she ages threatens her connectedness to life and her sense of self-worth.[9] Self-depreciation and despair among older women are often the result of no longer feeling needed. A number of older women tell me: "Nobody needs me." "I've got nobody." But the later years can have a positive as well as negative impact on woman's ethic of care. These years give women the opportunity to enlarge their circle of concern and free their activity of care from the wish for approval by others. This can deepen their personal integrity and strength. Mary appears in the Gospel as a woman of this kind of integrity. She cares for her son and his other followers in the days of derision and fear that accompany his death and burial, ignoring the disapproval of his enemies. Then she widens her responsibility and care to embrace the entire community of disciples.

The Gospel information on Mary is sparse. But what there is reveals the challenges and strengths of mature womanhood. As the contemporary poet May Sarton says in reflecting on Eve and Mary in "My Sisters, O My Sisters":

> For it is surely a lifetime work,
> This learning to be a woman.
> Until at the end what is clear
> Is the marvelous skill to make
> Life grow in all its forms.[10]

In the story of Mary we ponder the expanding circles of a woman's time, the need to understand and to live in charity during the dawning of new ages—and as Sarton says, the need "above all to be used fully, to be giving from wholeness, wholeness back to love's deep clarity." The whole of life is a journey toward old age, and from the perspective of faith, it is a journey toward wider circles of love.

## Naomi and Elizabeth: Older Women as Friends and Spiritual Guides

The Book of Ruth tells the story of a Hebrew woman, Naomi, who has moved to a foreign country, Moab, with her husband and two sons. There her sons marry Ruth and Orpah, women of Moab. In the course of the years, her husband and sons die, and Naomi, with little reason left to remain in a foreign land, decides to return to Bethlehem of Judah. This poses a dilemma for Ruth and Orpah, and they are torn between loyalty to their homeland and loyalty to their mother-in-law. Ruth selflessly follows Naomi. In Bethlehem Ruth meets and marries Boaz, a Hebrew kinsman of Naomi's, and she becomes the great-grandmother of David, Israel's greatest king.

The Book of Ruth can be read from many viewpoints. What interests us most here is the way it portrays friendship and loyalty between older and younger women. The two Moabite women, Orpah and Ruth, have obviously developed a deep affection for their mother-in-law Naomi. After the death of their husbands, both start out with Naomi on the road back to Judea (Ruth 1:7), and when Naomi tells them that for their own good they should each return to their mother's house, they both cry aloud and refuse. Orpah expresses no less loyalty than Ruth, although she does finally kiss her mother-in-law goodbye and return to her people.

What was it in Naomi that inspired such love and loyalty on the part of the two younger women? The story does not tell us. Their loyalty goes beyond all the demands of duty, and it is not something that could be taken for granted in the patriarchal society of the time. After Ruth and Naomi return to Judea, the other women in Naomi's home village appreciatively note Ruth's strong love and loyalty: "Your daughter-in-law . . . loves you and is more to you than seven sons" (Ru 4:15). Together Naomi and Ruth endure the emptiness of sorrow and loss. As Naomi says, "Filled full I departed, Yahweh brings me back empty" (1:21). Together they also experience the harvest and fullness that follows. The friendship clearly blesses both their lives.

Later, in Luke's Gospel, we discover another friendship between an older and younger woman which graces both lives. When Mary discovers that she is going to have a child, she goes as quickly as she can to a town in the hill country of Judah (Lk 1:39–56). She wants to share this news with her kinswoman Elizabeth. Luke has told us earlier that both Elizabeth and her husband Zechariah are getting on in years. When Mary greets her, Elizabeth learns not only that Mary is with child but also that Mary's child is the Messiah. Through their exchange both women receive a revelation of what God has done for the other, and they each rejoice in the gifts of God. They sing canticles of praise in response to the divine mercy. Elizabeth says to Mary: "Yes, blessed is she who believed that the promise made her by the Lord would be fulfilled" (1:45). Mary's canticle in response to Elizabeth's transfers this praise to God for the salvation that is unfolding: "My soul proclaims the greatness of the Lord and my spirit exalts in God my Savior" (1:46–55).

Luke tells us that Mary stayed with Elizabeth for three months before returning home (1:56). In this account of Mary's visit to Elizabeth we catch a glimpse of the way in which an older woman can be the spiritual friend of a younger woman. Such an exchange can be an occasion of joy and the deepening of faith. As with the visit of Mary and Elizabeth, both women come to understand better the workings of God in their lives. Many older women have what Anne Belford Ulanov calls "that inner order which produces a woman of great inward authority."[11] What characterizes these women is a willingness to let the divine into their lives. They then trust that life will flow through them to others; they are ready for bold action. Such women change the world around them through their impact on persons who come in contact with them. The Epistle to Titus recognizes this authority of older women, for it bids older women to teach others what is good (Ti 2:3).

These are some of the biblical women who give us glimpses of the strength and beauty of the older woman. Women, in general, in the New Testament remain closest to the death/resurrection mystery of Jesus. The women of Jerusalem meet Jesus as he carries his cross to the place of execution (Lk 23:26–32). Jesus affirms and supports women during his ministry, and they in turn remain with him to the bitter end, even when the other disciples have fled (Mk 15:40–41). The women disciples of Jesus stand by him through his death and burial (Lk 23:50–56). Women are also the initial witnesses of the resurrection. The risen Jesus appears first to Mary Magdalene and other women disciples. They are then sent to spread the good news of the resurrection (Mt 28:1–10).

These biblical women challenge the current stereotype of older women as used up and useless. Their beauty and influence increase rather than vanish with age. If older women are to give life to society today, they will need to remain close to the death/resurrection mystery which nourished the faith of New Testament women. For letting go of youthful images of beauty, especially those we cling to personally, means a kind of death. But as the Gospel tells us, such letting go is the way to new life. Like Martha, Anna, Mary, Naomi, and Elizabeth, contemporary older women have fresh images of beauty and mature gifts of faith to offer to Church and world. They are called to deliver that good news.

# 7

# HUMOR AND HOPE

In Chapter 18 of the Book of Genesis Sarah and Abraham entertain some unexpected guests. The biblical couple are well on in years, and it is the hottest part of the day. Nonetheless, when three men approach their tent at Mamre, Abraham rushes to get water and refreshments for them and Sarah begins to knead three bushels of flour into bread. When the guests are ready to leave, Sarah, listening at the entrance to the tent, hears them say that she and Abraham will have a son. She laughs. Can her barrenness really be turned to fullness? Is this emptiness she feels somehow a harbinger of hope?

The story of Sarah and Abraham is a tale of humor and hope. To older people who feel empty it presents the possibilities described in Psalm 92:14 of "still bearing fruit in old age, still remaining fresh and green." Welcome God with warm hospitality, the story says, and then expect things to happen through you which will be important for succeeding generations. Above all, refuse to believe that you are barren. Continue to laugh. The God who blessed Abraham and Sarah is still the ground of the future. Sarah and Abraham become models of faith because they know that the promises will be kept, even though they do not know what form that fulfillment will take.

And Sarah laughed. Humor should be a distinctive mark of the later years of life. Of course, we laugh from the time we are infants. We appreciate jokes, cartoons, and the incongruities of existence all our lives. But only when we have lived long enough to experience humanity in its range and complexity is our humor at its deepest and truest. Redemptive humor is more than the ability to enjoy an isolated humorous situation. It is an attitude toward all of life. Not only is humor a gift of the later years; it is indispensable to hope and healing during that time. Humor recognizes that limitations and failures are not final and unredeemable tragedies. Like a ray of sunshine piercing a dark and overcast sky, humor suggests God's abiding presence and brightens our human prospects.

Two themes found in the Genesis story of Abraham and Sarah are essential to a spirituality of the later years: humor and human limitation, and hope and human possibility. In a way, they are one theme, but we will look at each separately.

### Humor and Human Limitation

One day at a senior center I watched an elderly couple, heads bent over a piece of paper they were reading, laughing happily together. As I approached, the man was saying how he intended to send the piece to his children. They shared the copy with me, and I recognized it as a familiar anonymous piece called "A Senior's Lament." An excerpt from it reads:

> Everything is farther away than it used to be.
> It is twice as far to the corner, and they have added a
>    hill, I've noticed.

I have given up running for the bus.
It leaves faster than it used to.
It seems to me they are making the stairs steeper than
     in the old days, and have you noticed the smaller
     print they now use in the newspapers?
There is no sense in asking anyone to read aloud:
     Everyone speaks in such a low voice you can
     hardly hear them.

In one sense the piece is a description of the limitations of age. We slow down. Our senses lose some of their sharpness. Our energy level drops. We experience our finitude. Such experiences often bring us to the point of cynicism and hopelessness. But there is another dimension to the piece, captured by the laughter and delight of the couple I caught reading it. There is the humor which puts the whole thing in a different perspective, transforming our dismay into laughter. Humor recognizes the tragedy of the human condition, the finitude which in one way imprisons us. But by laughing at this condition, we declare that it is not final. It can be overcome. Humor is a gentle reminder of the reality of redemption.

Furthermore, laughter at its best is always social. A good joke cries out to be shared; it gets passed from person to person. More than that, humor is social because the joke is finally on all of us. Release and joy spring from genuine humor because we are acknowledging our infirmities and follies together. We are laughing not simply at our own condition but at the shared human condition. Such laughter is essential as we age, lest we become locked in our own isolation, and risk seeing our finitude as a personal problem separating us from others. One older man I know frequently greets his elderly friends by saying: "Well, I read the morning paper, and I didn't see my name in the obituaries, so I guess I must still be alive." They all laugh each time he says this, and suspend for a time some of their seriousness about the reality of death. At the same time, they feel a unity in their shared proximity to death.

We often describe those who are old as tough, as survivors. The Jewish writer Elie Wiesel writes how the fruit of Sarah and Abraham's faith, Isaac, teaches us how to survive. He calls the story of the sacrifice of Isaac, which occurs later in Genesis 22, "A Survivor's Story." It is a tale of fear and faith, defiance and laughter. Isaac is a survivor in a double sense. He is born against all odds, when Abraham and Sarah have no heir and are beyond their childbearing years. Then Abraham is asked to sacrifice this child of the promise, his only son. But tragedy is averted, and Isaac is restored to him. This ancient story, Wiesel says, is still our own, and every one of us will at one time or another be called to play a part in it. "Why," he asks, "was the most tragic of our ancestors named Isaac, a name which evokes and signifies laughter?" "Here is why," he says. "As the first survivor, he had to teach us, the future survivors of Jewish history, that it is possible to suffer and despair an entire lifetime and still not give up the art of laughter."[1]

The elderly know that tragedy and comedy belong together in life. They have lived long enough to finally understand the parable of the wheat and weeds. In that story from Matthew 13:24–30, a man sows good seed in his field. But while everyone is asleep, an enemy plants weeds among the wheat. The owner's servants want to know if they should try to root up the weeds that have grown up with the wheat. "No," the owner tells them, "because when you weed out the weeds you might pull up the wheat with it." A mixture of good and evil is inevitable in this life. Our successes are mixed with failures, our joys contain sadness, love can coexist with hate, health is marred by illness, and possessions are threatened by loss.

Because humor brings us back to earth, it helps us to use well what is left to us even when we are keenly aware of what we have lost or been denied. Only those who know how to weep can also laugh heartily; the pain of tragedy is preparation for the depth and breadth of comedy. Sarah's laughter has this quality; as we listen with her at the entrance to the tent, we are aware of the years of waiting and stigma she has experienced. As a man in his nineties once said to me: "I used to sing and laugh a lot when I was a child. Now I am coming back around to that place again, but with a difference. I laugh now in spite of all the pain I have known."

In *Naming the Whirlwind* Langdon Gilkey says that one of the joys of old age is the inner freedom no longer to expect too much of life.[2] This freedom does not negate a sense of caring. Rather, it encompasses those things we learn in maturity; such learning seldom involves information and skills. We learn not to use up energy in anxiety. We learn to live with things we cannot change. We learn that most people are neither for us nor against us but rather thinking about other matters. We learn that no matter how much we try to please, some people are never going to like us, a notion that troubles at first but is eventually quite a relief. In other words, inner freedom comes from acknowledging the limitations of life.

During the past decades many developmental thinkers have written about the mid-life crisis that occurs in our forties and fifties, describing it as a challenge to recognize the limits of our possibilities. Adrian Van Kaam refers to it as a transcendence crisis: "The midlife crisis is ultimately a spiritual one that challenges us to transcend a mainly vitalistic or functional appraisal of life." It implies an awareness of our mortality and finitude: "We begin to experience our human confinement in a way we can no longer deny; we do not feel as fit, as clever, or as effective as we used to."[3] In other words, we come up against the boundaries of our opportunities, our relationships, our strength and endurance, our dreams and ideals. This crisis is an invitation to become more aware of the transcendent dimension of life. It allows for a growth in wisdom and inwardness, for contact with our deepest self.

Since aging is a continuum, we must come to grips with limitations at every stage of the life cycle. Like the little girl who said, "This is the first time my mommie ever died," we learn very young that everything and everyone is finite. Losses make life contingent and unpredictable for all of us. The humor and hope of the elderly is a grace as we experience limitations. It says to persons of every age that these experiences need not diminish our human capacity for courage and love.

Because humor recognizes the limitations of human existence, it is also an antidote against setting up absolutes in life. One unattractive quality we can acquire as we age is a certain rigidity of spirit. Our ideas and values, habits and expectations, can become enshrined as gods. We find it easy to judge others harshly and difficult to make room for opinions and ideas different from our own. We see ours as the only way to be and to do. Humor can dissolve our pretense and illusions. As G. K. Chesterton put it, "Life is serious all the time, but living cannot be. You may have all the solemnity you wish in your neckties, but in anything important (such as sex, death, and religion), you must have mirth or you will have madness."[4] Laughter helps us relax and expand our vision.

Humor also opens us to the sacred. Since it both acknowledges our finiteness and at the same time transcends it, humor reveals that there is a *more* in the midst of human life.[5] It suggests the grace that grounds life, as the soft ripples on a river or the gentle breezes on a summer day are quiet reminders of greater depth and reality than we usually attend to. Humor reminds us that there is a larger perspective on life than our own.

Given the importance of humor to the experience of aging, what if we feel we have no sense of humor? Can we develop it? Try laughing. Make a cartoon of your present problem, and share it with others. Above all, try to be aware of the incongruities in life and in your own experience. Laughter often comes when we relax our defenses enough to see what was there all the time, though we hardly noticed it.

## Hope and Human Possibility

Humor is one way to acknowledge and transcend our limitations; hope is another. The Epistle to the Hebrews presents Sarah and Abraham as inspirations for all Christians because they have the kind of faith that sustains hope. They set out for the country that is their inheritance without knowing where they are going; they believe that the one who has made promises to them will be faithful. In other words, they trust that the future holds new possibilities for them. "Because of this, there came from one man, and one who was already as good as dead himself, more descendants than could be counted, as many as the stars of heaven or the grains of sand on the seashore" (Heb 11:12).

Hope lies at the center of every human life. Perhaps the most destructive thing our culture has done to the aging is to deprive them of hope by depicting the future as empty. Gabriel Marcel describes the effects of such an attitude.

To love anybody is to expect something from him, something which can neither be defined nor foreseen; it is at the same time in some way to make it possible for him to fulfil this expectation. Yes, paradoxical as it may seem, to expect is in some way to give: but the opposite is none the less true; no longer to expect is to strike with sterility the being from whom no more is expected; it is then in some way to deprive him or take from him in advance what is surely a certain possibility of inventing or creating.[6]

Studies suggest that a future orientation is critical to maintaining physical and mental health in mid- and late life. But often the future appears worse than empty to the aging; it looms as enemy. The future kills our plans, reveals our weakness, takes away our possessions, destroys our relationships, promises us death and perhaps a long and disabling illness on the way there.

In his *Images of Hope,* William Lynch emphasizes that hopelessness also springs from an overextension of hope.[7] By that he means an attitude which leaves no room for any expressions of discouragement, thus imposing an impossible ideal on persons. We expect one single, simple way of feeling in human situations; anger cannot coexist with love, nor despair with hope. This burdens people with a sense that they must have only beautiful feelings, leaving no room for the enormous rage that is buried within much sickness. If older persons say, "I feel weak," or "I do not think I will ever be completely free of this condition," we try to cheer them up. In so doing we nourish hopelessness by setting up an impossible ideal. A valid and honest hope must take account of the harsh realities we experience both personally and in our world.

In addition, some older people who are hardened by life limit hope in their own way. They do it in terms of their experience of what is possible in life; they have hoped before and been disappointed. The meaning of aging is really shaped in the imagination, for that is where we interpret the future. As Christians who are called to live by hope, we need to restore the sense that even as we age, the future is not only judgment, but also grace; it not only tears down, it also builds. In other words, the future need not be the path to despair; it can also lead to fresh blessings and achievements.

Through hope we expand the boundaries of what is possible in life. This quality of hope can perhaps be best seen in contrast with its opposite, hopelessness. What is this experience of hopelessness like? The most common images used to describe it are darkness, captivity, entrapment, a sense that there is no way out of a situation. Some older people I know give expression to it in phrases like, "What's the use?" "Nothing much will come of anything anyway." "I guess life is pretty much over for me." Hopelessness drains the energies of life. It is a sense of futility and apathy, a feeling that things are impossible and overwhelming. Then all life seems frozen, as by an early, bitter frost. In contrast, hope enables us to see things differently. We put the pieces of our life into a pattern never tried before. We insert something novel into the pattern or throw a new light on something old. As a bearer of hope, Jesus did this for those he met. Throughout the New Testament we see Jesus opening people's lives to a new freedom and a new future. G. K. Chesterton remarks that Jesus turned the world upside down, and when it was viewed from such a remarkable perspective, it suddenly made sense.

We do not often look to Jesus' life itself for clues to aging; perhaps that is because we see him cut off at the pinnacle of young adulthood. But there is a sense in which we can speak of the period of Jesus' public ministry as his later years. Christians have puzzled for generations over the length of time given to Jesus' hidden life, thirty years or so, in contrast to the brief period allotted to the more important tasks of preaching, teaching, working miracles, and shaping a group of disciples. Meditation on this ratio of years reveals the Christian call to regard the later years of life as filled with possibilities. No time is too short for the purposes of God. Jesus' last years numbered only three; for many older persons today, the later years number more like twenty-five to thirty. As a culture we are apt to disregard these years as no longer fruitful; the truth is closer to Jesus' witness that the fullness of our mission may await those years. We do not know what is our "hour," the time when events of most significance may occur in our lives. It may in fact be the final years, months, or moments of that life. A person with one hour to live can discover self and life in that hour and speak words to others which change lives. There are no deadlines on living, nor on what we may feel or do as long as we are alive.

Such an attitude requires the courage to begin anew, no matter what our age. Martin Buber writes of his encounter with the thinker Hans Natorp in the years immediately following the First World War.

At that time I was happily surprised at how the man with the steel-grey locks asked us at the beginning of his talk to forget all that we believed we knew about his philosophy from his books. In the last years, which had been war years, reality had been brought so close to him that he saw everything with new eyes and had to think in a new way. To be old is a glorious thing when one

has not unlearned what it means *to begin;* this old
man had even perhaps first learned it thoroughly
in old age.[8]

Buber himself illustrated this same ability to make a new
beginning. In spite of failing eyesight and repeated illness,
he continued work on his revision of the fourth edition of
his translation of the Hebrew Bible into German until he
entered his final coma. This willingness to begin anew may
mean taking up the writing of something one has set aside
for years, getting the college degree one has always wanted,
or beginning to paint or study music.

Beginning anew may also involve the discovery of elements of hope in an otherwise hopeless situation. In her
reflections on growing old creatively Sarah-Patton Boyle
tells how devastated she was initially by the realization that
her favorite cousin, Frank, had Alzheimer's disease. She
could not bear to witness the dimming of this shining mind;
Frank had such marvelous gifts of laughter, imagination,
appreciation, and affection. She writes that the first light-
ening of her darkness came with the slow realization that
seemingly senseless struggles are not, in fact, fruitless.

I was not successful in holding back the slow tide
of oblivion that engulfed Frank's mind. But my
attitude toward my role in his life was new. Now
I saw him as the giver, myself as his apprentice.
Instead of fighting to find strength and time to provide the emotional support, entertainment, and
exercise he needed, I found myself wondering
what I would learn from him that day. . . .

I could see also that the wiping away of memory
allowed him to experience long-familiar beauties

as though they were fresh from the hand of God. When we came on our walks to blooming honey-suckle, a bed of wild violets or a little waterfall, he would cry out like a child, "Oh, look at that!" as though nothing like it had ever been seen. Although the past faded with accelerating speed, his responses to the present moment were percep-tive and poetic.[9]

This is the way the unpredictable inbreaking of healing and new life came into one person's existence.

Christian hope lives in the matrix of faith. It is neither a magic formula, nor a naive optimism, nor a bargaining tool for a miraculous divine cure. Hope does not prescribe to God what is to be done in a particular situation. It does not, for example, identify physical recovery from an illness with salvation. Hope is open ended, based on trust that God's promises will be fulfilled. It provides a wider per-spective for all our limited hopes. Luke's story of the dis-ciples on the road to Emmaus depicts how such a destruc-tion of hope is prelude to the possibilities of God (Lk 24). As the story opens, we realize that it is spring in the land. Jerusalem is brimming with crowds celebrating Passover. Cleopas and his companion have turned their backs on this festive mood of the city and begun walking the seven miles back to the village of Emmaus. Nothing seems left to them; their leader has been strung on a cross outside the city walls. Their hearts and hopes are crushed. With downcast faces they pour out their story to the stranger who joins them, unaware that it is Jesus: "Our own hope had been that he would be the one to set Israel free." Jesus trans-forms their too circumscribed hopes by reinterpreting the events in Jerusalem, showing them that their hopes have indeed been fulfilled, but in a way beyond their expectations. More important, Jesus stays to break bread with them.

We cannot achieve hope alone. It is an act of communion. In other words, we create hope in one another. A member of the Pilgrim Place church-related retirement community in Claremont, California describes her own experience of this.

> We do a lot of laughing over here in the Pilgrim
> Place Retirement Community. We do it around
> those tables. That meal saves us. When Earl died,
> I walked over within twenty-four hours and I said,
> "Put me down for four days for the common
> meal." It saved my life.[10]

We give birth to hope in one another by offering help and by fostering the exploration of possibilities within ourselves and our situations.

Jesus gives us the Spirit as pledge and first fruits of our hope. Christian hope is a gift which we can refuse, but there is no indication that the gift ceases to be offered after a certain age. Paul says in his Letter to the Romans: "May the God of hope bring you such joy and peace in your faith that the power of the Holy Spirit will remove all bounds to hope" (15:13). In fact, Luke describes the outpouring of the Spirit at Pentecost as resulting in new wellsprings of creativity specifically for the old. Quoting a passage from the prophet Joel, he says of this coming of God's Spirit,

> In the days to come—it is the Lord who speaks—
> I will pour out my spirit on all humankind.
> Your sons and daughters shall prophesy,

> your young men shall see visions,
> your old men shall dream dreams (Acts 2:17).

The biblical God is throughout a God of the future, leading all into the new, regardless of age.

The later years may in fact be especially attuned to the experience of hope. Old age has been described as a time when being becomes more important than having or doing. The philosopher Gabriel Marcel believes that such freedom from having is especially conducive to the existence of hope. This is so because divine hope is characterized by a certain light-heartedness in life, an attitude destroyed by the gnawing anxiety which accompanies a preoccupation with having.

> If, however feebly, we remain penetrated by hope,
> it can only be through the cracks and openings
> which are to be found in the armour of having
> which covers us: the armour of our possessions,
> our attainments, our experience and our virtues,
> perhaps even more than our vices.[11]

The emptying out which is usually a part of growing old makes room for God.

The Christian's final hope is based on communion, a union with God which is indestructible. Even in situations where we do not tangibly experience God's support, impossible situations without a glimmer of hope, even in these dark nights of faith we believe that God is near at hand. This is what is revealed in the resurrection of Jesus; death cannot sever our bond with God. All our smaller hopes are drawn from this one large hope. Yet Christian hope will often stand in contradiction to reality as we experience it. Death remains death, and suffering is a cry of the human heart to which there is no easy answer. Jesus based his hope on the unshakable conviction that God's power was at work in the world and that the reign of God would finally appear in its fullness. He hoped sufficiently in God not to try to hasten the reign of God by changing stones into bread or becoming the kind of political Messiah the crowds expected. The Christian moves through suffering, guilt, and death where in fact they have been broken through—that is, in the raising of the crucified Jesus. And as the German theologian Jürgen Moltmann emphasizes in his *Theology of Hope,* "Hope finds in Christ not only a consolation *in* suffering, but also the protest of the divine promise *against* suffering."[12] Christian hope is not a private hope for a hereafter; instead, it is an expression of love and unity with all who suffer. By opening ourselves to the promises of God, we become, like Sarah and Abraham, bearers of that promise for all succeeding generations.

# *8*

# **LOSS**

My grandmother, Mary Volk, died several years ago at the age of eighty-seven. She was my lifelong friend, and taught me many important lessons. Mary immigrated to South Dakota as a child, part of a group of Germans who left Odessa, Russia when Czar Alexander II, a great-grandson of Catherine the Great, desired to modernize his empire by implementing a series of sweeping reforms. Later Mary and her husband brought their family to Salem, Oregon after the government foreclosed the mortgage on their Dakota farm.

Mary was a staunch Catholic, finding sustenance in her daily rosary and the devotional life of the Church. During her later years she lived in a small white house across the street from the parish church and school. Here she could make her way to Mass and mark her hours by the voices of children dismissed for recess or the end of the school day.

Toward the end of her life it became necessary to move Mary to a nursing home. Though she had set out before for new lands, this journey to the nursing home was the most difficult exodus of all. When I visited her there she would frequently say to me, "Something is wrong deep down in my heart, and I don't know what it is." She lived in the nursing home as in a foreign land, and when she showed me around it was always with the attitude of a visitor who was just passing through. Mary's struggle to absorb the losses that accompanied the last years of her life was indeed like that of Israel's exile in Babylon.

Dealing with loss is one of the great spiritual challenges of aging. Losses occur throughout our lives, but they often come at a faster pace in the last years. Older persons have more chronic illnesses and suffer more acute and chronic pain than younger persons. They visit doctors and are hospitalized twice as often, and stay twice as long.[1] Hearing and sight dim. Retirement may mean separation from the work that gave life meaning. And perhaps the deepest loss of all is the death of a lifelong friend or spouse. In her novel *Autumn*, A. G. Mojtabai captures well the emotional levels of such loss. The novel tells the story of Will, a recent widower in his late sixties, who settles in for autumn in the small Maine town where he and his wife Helen had hoped to spend their last years together. Now Will faces the winter alone. He is bewildered and angry at the prospect of being old and by himself.

> I stand, look out, see water, see ridges on the water, see nothing. The day shuts down. Someone touches my hand—it's nothing. A leaf maybe, a skip of the wind, a wish—you are five months gone.[2]

Will wonders why there are so many stories for growing up and none for growing down. Nothing speaks to him. He balls up a second pillow at night and hugs it close, making believe that it is a shoulder—no one's in particular. He asks only that it be a warm one.

We are required to make more changes during our last years than at any other period in our lives, and these changes inevitably involve some loss. Such losses are especially hard because we have devoted most of our days to acquiring the very things that are now disappearing: friends, a wife or husband, children, a home, a job, financial security. The time left to us seems too short to replace any of them.

Moreover, these losses are an assault on our feelings of self-worth. We grieve not only for our losses, but for the ultimate loss of self. Spouse and friends are part of who we are, and when they are gone, we feel pared down; part of us is missing. One woman in her seventies who began to eat constantly when she lost her husband and two close friends said to me, "I'm not really hungry. I can't be; just empty, I guess." Another woman who had spent thirty years doing piece work in a garment factory was laid off quite unexpectedly when she was sixty-seven. The owners had promised her that she would be able to work for several more years, but the firm ran into financial difficulties and was unable to honor the promise. "Do you know what it is like," she asked, "to suddenly find that you have no reason at all to get up in the morning?" She was strong and in very good health, but could find no meaning for her existence.

Some losses that presently accompany aging may be lessened or even eliminated in the future. The medical sciences predict a healthier old age as diseases now confused with the process of aging are cured. There may be major breakthroughs, for example, in the treatment of cancer, stroke, and heart disease. Victories against age discrimination in the job market could allow older persons to continue working longer at jobs of their choice. We do not yet know what aging would look like if our society really supported and valued it. We must do whatever we can to reduce the losses that are now a part of aging. At the same time, we know that loss will continue to mark the later years of life, as it does all stages of human growth. At certain points in all of our lives we are faced with crises which can only be resolved by letting go of past forms. Either that, or we stagnate in a fixation on the past.

How we deal with the experience of loss is one of the most critical factors in our happiness or unhappiness as we age. As Carl Jung has said, we cannot live the evening of life in the same manner as the morning.[3] We need spiritual resources to guide us through the transition. One of the biblical stories that can provide such help is the account of Israel's experience of exile. We will listen to three moments in that story which are particularly important for understanding and living through losses with faith: (1) a new song in a foreign land, (2) every morning God's mercies are new, and (3) God will never forget you.

## A New Song in a Foreign Land

In the sixth century B.C. the Israelites find themselves a defeated nation, exiled to Babylonia on the banks of the river Chebar. In some ways life is not too hard on them; they have freedom to move about and to earn a living. But when news of the destruction of Jerusalem and the temple arrives, the exiles are too stunned and shocked to know how to react. They have lost the land which was the inheritance God promised them. Now the temple of Jerusalem, the place where Yahweh dwelt in their midst, has been burned down. They are bereft in an alien land: "By the streams of Babylon we sat and wept when we remembered Zion" (Ps 137:1). The collapse of their most important symbol systems, land, monarchy, temple, and independence, creates a situation of deep homelessness.

The Babylonians chide the exiles and ask them to sing a song to Yahweh now, if they have heart. The Israelites wonder how they can sing to a God who has let them down, in a land not their own: "How could we sing a song to the Lord in a foreign land?" (Ps 137:4). Some of the people turn to the prophet Ezekiel who is with them in exile and cry out, "How can we survive?" (Ez 33:10). The Israelites find their old identity crushed, and they search for a new one. "How can we live? Who are we now?" they wonder.

Israel learns that her survival depends on learning to sing her old song in a new way. In other words, she must let go of former ways of understanding God's presence and allow the symbols of her faith to be transformed. In this way she can retain her identity and find God even in Babylon. One of our most vivid images of the movement from loss to new life comes from this period in Israel's history. It is the vision of the dry bones found in Ezekiel 37:1–14. The prophet Ezekiel sees a plain filled with dry bones. His vision symbolizes the despair of Israel. She is dead as a community and as an historical power, crying out: "Our bones are dried up, our hope is lost, and we are cut off" (v. 11). Standing in this valley of death's shadow, Ezekiel is asked, "Can these bones come to life?" "Lord God," he replies, "you alone know that."

The answer Ezekiel receives in the valley of dry bones is that the future of his people, the movement from death to new life, rests upon the gift of God's Spirit. It is this gift that will make possible new beginnings, inward and outward survival. Along with the prophet Jeremiah, Ezekiel insists that external conditions are important, but what God will bring about in the heart of the people is even more important. The old symbols of exodus, land, and temple must be transformed and given a new meaning. Deeper than that, God will create a new identity and center of loving belief: "I will give you a new heart and place a new spirit within you, taking from your bodies your stony hearts and giving you natural hearts" (Ez 36:26). Israel learned that her hope rested in the presence of God, but she could not prescribe to God what was to be done. It was not her place to program the specific actions of God. Israel did not get Jerusalem and the temple back in the way she had known them. She was given instead an inner and deeper gift.

One can, of course, be in exile without ever leaving the land; exile is not simply a matter of geographical separation. It is a state of being, a state of the spirit. And the key to happiness as we age lies in the same lesson Israel learned in the exile. We must undergo a conversion, an experience of losing our song in order to be able to sing it again in a new key. Even though the melodies of our life will not be played again in the same way, we must not close the keyboard and allow it to gather dust. One woman showed me how beauty and new life can arise from a positive attitude toward loss. Before I knew her story, what struck me most about her was the warmth of her outreach toward others. Later she told me that she had had a serious stroke which meant learning to talk all over again and getting around in a wheelchair. She even had to relearn the alphabet. What helped her do this, she said, was taking one day at a time and concentrating on what she still had left, especially her ability to love and to listen to others. Out of that experience had come a new appreciation of the gift of communication and a quiet courage, gifts she now shared with many.

As with Israel, the Spirit of God is the source of our ability to replace what is lost with something new in our lives. But like Israel, we must let go of some aspects of our past if we are to move to a new level of living. Aging calls for a revision of values. If, for example, we continue to see income and power as the criteria for our personal value, we will never discover other sources of self-worth. The American playwright Arthur Miller shows us how difficult it can be to go against cultural forces which influence our sense of identity. In *Death of a Salesman,* the main character, Willy Loman, reaches for images that cannot bring him happiness. He is seduced into focusing on competition and success, but discovers as he ages that no one will buy. He is in pain, but cannot find the reasons for his distress. Limited by his competitive perspective, he does not ask whether success can be defined in other than financial terms.

Insisting on the same activities and schedules we've always known will prevent us from finding new ones when our energy level keeps us from repeating the old. Denying that we are growing old will stop us from turning it into a positive experience. An eighty-one year old woman with whom I worked was having increasing difficulty walking and seeing. She insisted, however, that this was simply the result of her inability to get a good night's sleep, and she refused to acknowledge that she was experiencing some physical loss as a result of aging. She remained irritable and angry, closed to all efforts of those who loved her to take positive steps to help her compensate for the losses in sight and mobility. Her denial blocked the joy and satisfaction she might have continued to experience from those relationships.

On the other hand, openness to the gift of the Spirit enables us to admit that aging does involve some loss. We can then adapt accordingly, whether that means wearing a hearing aid, traveling by taxi rather than driving ourselves, finding satisfaction in giving joy and pleasure to others, developing an unknown or unused talent, or looking for new friends and interests when we have lost old ones. For example, if we are willing to acknowledge some loss of physical strength and stamina, we may find that the experience accruing from longer living can enable us to accomplish more than when we were young, but by a different means. Learning to define comfort and happiness in terms of satisfying human relationships or creative spiritual activities can help us cope with the loss of physical well-being. Perhaps an even more difficult conversion may also be asked of us, a change in attitudes which we held earlier in life, but which are now seen to be too competitive, jealous, or overly ambitious. Research shows that failure to allow this sort of transformation of our values, interests, and activities is one of the major causes of unhappiness during the later years.[4]

The exiles found it difficult to sing old songs in a foreign land. Their experience is illumined in the works of the contemporary Jewish writer, Elie Wiesel. In *Ani Maamin* he tells of a song that was lost and found again.[5] It is an old song about a messiah and his failure to appear, a despairing yet hopeful song which he has recovered from his Hasidic childhood. Though it is at times tearful, the song is finally full of a veiled but visible hope which enables us to face the future in spite of all heartaches. "Ani Maamin" are the first words of one of the thirteen articles of faith: "I believe in the coming of the messiah." Wiesel sang the words as a young Hasidic Jew and believed them. Later he heard the song sung in the death camps and wondered how it could continue to be sung in circumstances like these. But even in the midst of this suffering he finds experiences of presence and hope: there is a suffering child who believes, a Jew in a doomed village who suddenly sings of his ancient and lost faith, and an inmate in the death camp who affirms that, even there, he will wait for the messiah to come.

I shall wait for you.
And even if you disappoint me
I shall go on waiting.

It is with songs that are lost and found again that the story of God's people continues to be sung.

## Every Morning God's Mercies Are New

The most important adjustment that the exiles in Babylon must make is a religious one. In spite of the loss of land and temple, they are asked to continue to believe that the God who was with them in those embodiments is still with them even though those particualr embodiments are gone. During this time many of the prayers found in the Book of Psalms were brought together. They express two aspects of the experience of loss: (1) the anger and grief that accompany mourning, and (2) the conviction that God's love is certain and durable.

The Book of Lamentations consists of five poems which come from early in the exile. In them the author articulates his grief over many aspects of this devastation. The first lamentation begins:

> Oh, how lonely she sits,
>> the city once thronged with people,
> As if suddenly widowed.
>> Though once great among the nations,
> She, the princess among provinces,
>> is now reduced to vassalage.
>
> She passes her nights weeping;
>> the tears run down her cheeks (1–2).

We need to grieve for our losses. Acknowledging the loss allows us to experience a whole range of emotions and to share the pain with others. Prayer lets us share this grief with God, knowing that God is on our side in the struggle with pain and suffering. Anger and guilt often accompany the experience of loss. We may be angry at the deceased person for leaving us, angry at ourselves or at doctors, angry at God for allowing this separation in our lives. Often this anger is at root an expression of loneliness and fear. Sometimes loss also gives rise to false guilt; we wonder if we are being punished for something we did in our life. One woman asked if she was losing her sight because she had disobeyed her mother and read in the dark when she was a child; another man thought that the loss of his job meant that he had not trusted God enough. The prayers of the exiles freely express before God these intense and often contradictory emotions that follow a loss such as the death of a spouse or friend: "My way is hid from the Lord, and my night is disregarded by my God" (Is 40:27). They reflect a trust that God is large enough to handle our anger and fear.

The Psalms do not deal in vague generalities. They enumerate the sufferings of the speakers in concrete and passionate detail: "I am like a dish that is broken." (Ps 31:13). They work their way through these emotions before they come at the end to an underlying note of hope and trust. Psalm 13 reveals the pattern of such grieving in faith.

How much longer will you forget me, Yahweh?
Forever?
How much longer will you hide your face from me?
How much longer must I endure grief in my soul,
and sorrow in my heart by day and by night? . . .
But I for my part rely on your love, Yahweh;
let my heart rejoice in your saving help (1–5).

Another example of this movement through grief to hope is found in Psalm 42. This lament is a profound expression of longing for the divine presence, and a stirring recital of human grief and pain.

> Why so downcast, my soul,
>     why do you sigh within me?
> Put your hope in God: I shall praise him yet,
>     my savior, my God (5–6).

Like the other laments, Psalm 42 mirrors a spirit unafraid to speak to God of *all* the emotions and questions, even the deeply negative ones, which accompany grieving. At the same time it reveals trust that healing will come in its time. Not even death can sever the communion of God's people with their God.

The Psalms are among the favorite prayers of many older people, and perhaps the one most frequently prayed is Psalm 23.

> Even though I walk in the dark valley
>     I fear no evil; for you are at my side
> With your rod and your staff
>     that give me courage (4).

The Psalms reflect a people's growing realization that they can turn to God anywhere with confidence. God is near and is their strength even in a foreign land. The one thing that gives hope to the poet of Lamentations, that on which alone he sets his heart, is that God's mercies never come to an end. The gracious kindnesses of God are not worn out or used up; they are new every morning (3:22; Jb 29:20). The final resolution of the crisis of exile is trust in the faithfulness of God. When God seems most hidden—there, in exile—the people speak of God's revelation.

Such honest prayer of grieving in the face of loss helps us move to new levels of faith and healing. It is also an experience which prepares the elderly for one of their important ministries within the community of faith. Because they know loss so deeply and in its multiple forms, older persons are especially well equipped to minister to those of any age who experience loss and are searching for hope again: the young child whose favorite pet is killed, the teenager whose love ends in disappointment, the young father who loses a job and agonizes over supporting a family, the adult woman who finds it hard to see her children leave home. Grief is an intrinsic part of human experience. Throughout life we know not just large griefs such as divorce, loss of health, or the death of loved ones, but also the small griefs of change of jobs or schools, disappointment in friendships and failure in projects. At these times older persons who have themselves walked through the valley of darkness can be compassionate guides for others who must find their way in the same valley. By their continued faith in the face of loss, they assure us that God's mercies are in fact new every morning.

## God Will Never Forget You

For the ancient Hebrew, the ultimate loss was to be forgotten, erased from the memory of family and tribe, and from the memory of God. If God forgets you, it is as though you never existed. We share this concern of the ancient Hebrews. The philosopher Alfred North Whitehead believes that the deepest religious yearning of humankind is for an order of existence in which newness does not mean loss: "The world is thus faced by the paradox that ... it craves for novelty and yet is haunted by terror at the loss of the past, with its familiarities and its loved ones."[6] For

Whitehead, the ultimate expression of evil is found in the fact that the past fades; change means a perpetual perishing which threatens to rob experiences of their significance. Aging is an experience of temporality, and we have come to view temporality as continual loss. Joys and beauty fade with time; success does not last. Whatever our age, the passage of time can undermine our achievements and threaten our relations. It evokes anxiety and fear. There is a universal longing which finds expression in the religious question: Is there any permanent meaning to my life in this world?

Among the older persons who seem especially forgotten by God are those with forms of dementia, such as Alzheimer's disease. This is a loss particularly painful for friends and relatives of the afflicted person. A son writes of his mother:

> My mother used to be God's good friend. She prayed to him three times a day, as a devout Jew should. She cared for her mentally ill sister and was a faithful visitor to the sick and the dying. God has become a stranger to her, as have all her old friends. She mentions his name from time to time, as if wondering what became of him. He seems as hard for her to locate these days as a hair pin.[7]

In *The Summer of the Great Grandmother,* Madeleine L'Engle also reflects on what the loss of her mother's memory means for both of them. She finds help in affirming her belief in God's memory of her mother. If God is a God worth believing in, she concludes, then he is a loving God who will not abandon or forget the smallest atom of creation, including her mother.[8]

In the midst of the exile, Israel's experience of loss also leads her to wonder if God has forgotten her. But the prophets declare that God remembers her everlastingly.

> For Zion was saying, "Yahweh has abandoned me,
>     the Lord has forgotten me."
> Does a woman forget her baby at the breast,
>     or fail to cherish the son of her womb?
> Yet even if these forget,
>     I will never forget you (Is 49:14–15).

Reflection on the losses connected with aging pushes us back to this same concern with the preservation of our life and values in God.

In his writings Whitehead describes God as the Final Wisdom. When this image is unfolded, it becomes a way of affirming Isaiah's statement that God will not forget us. Process theologians, building on Whitehead's insights, speak of God as responsive love. This means that our joys and actions matter in the divine life itself. Our values and achievements are taken up and endure in the continuing life of God. The solution to our fear of temporality does not lie in God's eternity, but rather in God's real relationship to the world. God is involved in time, and is enriched by what happens in the world. God constantly receives from the world and retains what in the world has passed beyond its present immediacy. God knows every reality precisely as it experienced itself, including its experience of temporality, "its suffering, its sorrows, its failures, its triumphs, its immediacies of joy."[9] God experiences *this* world as it is.

God integrates this reality into the divine harmony and, in light of it, continually offers redemption to the world. Over against the waste and tragedy in life, there is a renewing power at work. God's wisdom is faithful and creative, ever offering us new possibilities according to our total situations. The past is both preserved and transformed in this wisdom which overcomes the final evil of our temporal existence. This conviction was also central to the vision of Teilhard de Chardin.

> A thought, a material improvement, a harmony, a unique nuance of human love, the enchanting complexity of a smile or a glance, all these new beauties that appear for the first time, in me or around me, on the human face of the earth—I cherish them like children and cannot believe that they will die entirely in their flesh. If I believed that these things were to perish forever, should I have given them life? The more I examine myself, the more I discover this psychological truth: that no one lifts his little finger to do the smallest task unless moved, however obscurely, by the conviction that he is contributing infinitesimally (at least indirectly) to the building of something definitive—that is to say, to your work, my God.[10]

Recognition of God as Final Wisdom supports our hope that the future will embody our creative gifts, even if the particular use of these gifts may not be what we anticipate; they may, in fact, be used in an unexpectedly creative manner.

Whitehead also speaks of God as everlasting. As the immediate moments of our existence are transformed in God's life, our present actions pass into permanent significance. God receives into the divine life every actuality in its own uniqueness and individuality. This everlasting reality is the Kingdom of heaven. God's tender care and infinite patience concern themselves that nothing be lost which can be saved, even what the world might consider "mere wreckage."[11] These images recall that of the poet Gerard Manley Hopkins who asks in "The Leaden Echo and the Golden Echo" if there is no way to keep beauty from vanishing. Hopkins concludes that in God

> the thing we freely forfeit is kept
>     with fonder a care,
> Fonder a care kept than we could have kept it. . . . [12]

In describing God's saving care, Whitehead says that God preserves what is worth preserving; what is trivial is relegated to triviality. In spite of the waste in the world, what is past is not finally lost, but is recognized everlastingly in God. As the prophet Isaiah affirmed, God will not forget us; our lives are safe in God. We contribute not only to our own and others' enjoyment, but everlastingly to the joy of God. This gives an ultimate ground to our hope.

As we deal with the losses of aging, the story of Israel's exile can enlighten and strengthen us. From that story we can learn to sing a new song, to believe in the mercy of God, and to trust that God is everlasting and will not forget us.

# 9

# DYING

"It's not death I fear," a man in his seventies told me, "it's all that I might have to go through before it comes." An older woman, who had just been told by her doctor that she had cancer, said to me: "You know, at my age I have pretty much come to terms with death. I figure I have lived a long and quite satisfying life. But I do not know what lies ahead, and I am afraid of the possible suffering and pain. Will I be able to deal with them?" What both of these older people were articulating is the difference between death and dying. Death is the final moment of life, the end of life as we know it. Dying, on the other hand, is the journey a person must take in the last phase of life. It is the process leading to the end, and for older persons it can sometimes be a long journey of progressive suffering on many levels. They often fear weakness, pain, physical dependence, and mental deterioration more than the cessation of life. Death itself is then longed for as a release from a dying process that seems endless and senseless.

Both death and dying can occur at any age. But when death comes at the end of a long life, it is more likely to be preceded by the period of diminishment and decline we call dying. The movement from life to death extends into a longer slope. Decline is no longer temporary, able to be

overcome; it now seems inevitable. As T. S. Eliot's Prufrock says:

> I have seen the moment of my greatness flicker,
> And I have seen the eternal Footman hold my coat,
>    and snicker,
> And in short, I was afraid.[1]

A spirituality for the later years must therefore come to
terms with this concluding phase of life. It requires a theology of dying. In this chapter we will explore the suggestions provided for such a theology in three sources: (1)
Paul's Second Letter to the Corinthians, (2) the writings of
Teilhard de Chardin, and (3) the sacrament of anointing of
the sick. All three show that dying in imitation of Christ
demands the surrender of one's life in order to gain it afresh
as God's gift. The chapter will conclude with a brief reflection on the right to die.

### Dying and New Existence in Christ:
### Paul's Second Letter to the Corinthians

Paul wrote his Second Letter to the Corinthians about
56 A.D. from a town in Macedonia. It is intensely personal,
filled with many paradoxes. In one of the early chapters of
this epistle, while pondering the paradox that life somehow
comes through death, Paul makes a statement that could be
seen as a description of the dying process. Paul says: "That
is why there is no weakening on our part, and instead,
though this outer person of ours may be falling into decay,
the inner person is renewed day by day" (2 Cor 4:16).

At first glance Paul seems to be using the phrases
"outer person" and "inner person" to refer to body and
spirit, and to be saying that though our body is declining,

our spirit is growing. However, this would not be in keeping with Paul's view of the human person, for he does not think in terms of a body/spirit split, but rather of the whole person, a unity of body and spirit. His meaning is somewhat more complex, but very important for understanding the dying that takes place in the later years.

Paul is talking about two kinds of personal existence. When he speaks of the "outer person" he means our whole self insofar as it is subject to the troubles and diminishments of this world. It is human existence still under the power of sin, suffering, and decay. This "outer person" is wasting away; its dissolution has its completion in death. The "inner person" is the existence we will know fully in the age to come. But this inward or new person does not belong only to the future; renewal is taking place day by day in this world for the person united with Christ. Such renewal is an anticipation of the future which will bring the promised new Spirit and a new heart. The age to come is already partially present. There is a competing power already at work negating death because of the resurrection of Jesus. It is destroying the old order and unleashing new patterns of possibility. In faith we believe that this is true even when we experience very little evidence that any inner renewal is taking place. In a process begun on earth and continued after death, Christ in some way already shares with his followers his own life and personality: "He will transfigure the body belonging to our humble state, and give it a form like that of his own resplendent body" (Phil 3:21). This hope is the result of our union with Christ; Christ and his followers are so vitally united that he shares his triumph over death with them.

Paul sees the resurrection principle already at work in Christ's followers by the power of the Spirit who dwells in them: while the "outward person" wastes away, this new existence is already taking shape. Some of the benefits of this new age may be enjoyed in the present. Jesus' followers may already perceive the world in a new light and "walk in the newness of life" (Rom 6:4). The late Rabbi Abraham Heschel filled out the meaning of Paul's words when, speaking at the 1961 White House Conference on Aging, he referred to old age as a time not of stagnation, but of opportunities for personal growth.

> The years of old age may enable us to attain the high values we failed to sense, the insights we have missed, the wisdom we ignored. They are indeed formative years, rich in possibilities to unlearn the follies of a lifetime, to see through in-bred self-deceptions, to deepen understanding and compassion, to widen the horizon of honesty, to refine the sense of fairness.[2]

In light of Paul's words, such growth would be an expression of the life of the Spirit within, evidence that the power of the new age is already at work in us. Weakness can be the very occasion in which power paradoxically expresses itself: "We are only the earthenware jars that hold this treasure, to make it clear that such an overwhelming power comes from God and not from us" (2 Cor 4:8). It depends on our response to the love and grace poured forth by the Spirit into our hearts (Rom 5:5).

Earlier in his Second Letter to the Corinthians Paul reminds us that the Christian life is a continuous process of self-identification with Christ. He says that "we carry with us in our body the death of Jesus, so that the life of Jesus, too, may always be seen in our body" (2 Cor 4:10). The Corinthians to whom Paul is writing want instant glory; Paul says that it comes as we share in Christ's sufferings.

Christian discipleship means union with the crucified Lord. Such suffering, like Christ's, can be redemptive. It may be that one of the gifts of the elderly to the Christian community is to fully and visibly witness to this pattern of Christian existence which is marked by suffering and death on the one hand and divine strength on the other, a dialectic of weakness, dying and death on the one hand and power and resurrection on the other.

Such dying with Christ may be experienced as the pressing in of non-existence. For many, it is like the entrance into the dark night of the soul or the cloud of unknowing described by mystics like John of the Cross. This process of dying to self and entry into the world of the new has been described in another way in Bernadette Roberts' *The Experience of No-Self*. Roberts tells of the loneliness of the loss of self experienced in her contemplative journey. She finds her experience shared by a woman nearly forty years older than she is, her eighty-five year old friend Lucille.

> On my way to the library one afternoon, I stopped by Lucille's house to see if she might be taking her daily walk in my direction. While getting her things together she casually asked me, "So what's new?" I replied, "I don't have a self anymore." She turned to me with a bemused smile, "You, of all people! No self?" and broke into such a hearty laughter that I had to steady her on her feet. When she stopped laughing she asked, "Now tell me, seriously, what does this mean—you have no self?" I told her I didn't know, which was why I was on my way to the library, to find out. Then she began laughing all over again, and her laughter

was infectious: after all, what could be more absurd than losing your self?

As we walked along I told her about this unusual state and described some of its effects. At one point she stopped walking and turned to me. "You know," she said, "I recognize what you are describing, but I'm wondering how you know all this, because you are too young. What you are talking about is the aging process. It is a change of consciousness that is reserved for the final years. It is the last stage in life, a getting ready for a new existence—and you're too young![3]

Perhaps this experience points in another way to what Paul meant when he said that our outer self is dying while our inner self is growing strong; the former identity is giving way, while a new existence is beginning to break through.

### Redemptive Diminishment:
### The Writings of Teilhard de Chardin

A number of persons find their spirituality nourished in the later years by the writings of the Jesuit paleontologist and religious thinker, Teilhard de Chardin. Two of his themes, redemptive diminishment and the spiritualization of matter, are especially pertinent to the process of decline frequently experienced in these years.

In *The Divine Milieu* Teilhard notes that the passivities of life comprise more than half our total existence. These passivities are the things that are undergone by us, in contrast to the things we actively do. Although we view the active realm as more important, the passive is immeasurably the wider and deeper part of life. These forces which press in upon us can be either friendly or hostile, either passivities of growth or passivities of diminishment. As Teilhard says, "we undergo life as much as we undergo death."[4] Our self is given to us far more than it is formed by us.

It is easier to accept the passivities of growth, the gifts of life given us by others and the universe itself. The challenge is to somehow find God in the midst of the vast, varied and constant passivities of diminishment: the crushing failure, the barrier blocking our way, the sudden accident or illness.

> And if by chance we escape, to a greater or lesser extent, the critical forms of these assaults from without which appear deep within us and irresistibly destroy the strength, the light and the love by which we live, there still remains that slow, essential deterioration which we cannot escape: old age little by little robbing us of ourselves and pushing us on towards the end.[5]

Death is the sum and consummation of all our diminishments. It is also a critical point on the road to union.

Teilhard seeks to find God even in these diminishments. Doing so means moving through two phases. We must first struggle against them; only then can they become redemptive. Diminishments are evil, and God wants us free of them. Our first act is therefore to resist evil, to do all within our power to see that nothing of value within or around us is destroyed, to regard our search for comfort and healing as inspired by God. Reducing pain whenever possible and fostering research that will put an end to the diseases common in old age are ways of siding with God against the destructive diminishments of aging. The Southern fiction writer, Flannery O'Connor, who died of lupus

when she was only thirty-nine, was very moved by Teilhard's writings on diminishment. She described his idea to
a friend as "those afflictions that you can't get rid of and
have to bear. Those that you can get rid of he believes you
must bend every effort *to* get rid of."[6]

However great our resistance to the forces of diminishment, there nonetheless comes a point when we gradually
feel them gaining the ascendancy. Then, and only then,
does Teilhard speak of their capacity for being transformed
into good. This is especially true of the diminishments we
have described as the process of dying; in the last stages of
life we sometimes experience losses which do not include
any perceptible advantages, and weaknesses which affect
the deepest reaches of our being.

> When the signs of age begin to mark my body (and
> still more when they touch my mind); when the ill
> that is to diminish me or carry me off strikes from
> without or is born within me; when the painful
> moment comes in which I suddenly awaken to the
> fact that I am ill or growing old; and above all at
> that last moment when I feel I am losing hold of
> myself and am absolutely passive within the
> hands of the great unknown forces that have
> formed me; in all those dark moments, O God,
> grant that I may understand that it is you (pro-
> vided only my faith is strong enough) who are
> painfully parting the fibres of my being in order to
> penetrate to the very marrow of my substance and
> bear me away within yourself.[7]

Teilhard prays that he may see death as an act of communion. Union always means dying partially in order to
achieve union with what one loves. We relinquish previous

convictions in order to embrace a new idea. We risk being changed when we enter into a close friendship. So, too, there is a tearing up of our roots, a loss of self, involved in our journey to God.

In addition to these reflections on diminishment, a second theme in Teilhard's writings, the spiritualization of matter, is pertinent to the process of dying. Sometimes aging is experienced as a decline in our physical being, just as we are on the verge of understanding some of the more important truths of life. One woman put it rather graphically: "I was just fine until I reached my seventies; then there was a tinkling and a rattling, and my body simply fell apart." Florida Scott-Maxwell describes this same paradox in a slightly different way.

> Age puzzles me. I thought it was a quiet time. My seventies were interesting, and fairly serene, but my eighties are passionate. I grow more intense as I age. To my own surprise I burst out with hot conviction. Only a few years ago I enjoyed my tranquillity; now I am so disturbed by the outer world and by human quality in general that I want to put things right, as though I still owed a debt to life. I must calm down. I am far too frail to indulge in moral fervour.[8]

Just when our spirit longs to create something that transcends time, our body seems to break down. What can be said of this uneven decline of inner and outer powers?

In Teilhard's view of the world, evolution involves the gradual spiritualization of matter. For Teilhard, matter and spirit are not too different realities, but the without and the within of all things. Throughout the entire process of evolution matter has been furling in on itself, interiorizing itself. Teilhard does not think that matter is unimportant; his is not a dualistic system of thought. Rather, what he calls spirit is really a highly complex form of matter. What is of value in the material world becomes spiritualized during a lifetime. For Teilhard evolution is, in fact, a process where the dominance of the without, or matter, gives way to the dominance of the within, or spirit. In his vision of the future, spirit will rise to divine union, and the remnant that remains of the material will sink back into chaos: "Spirit is the extract of the universe, like a precious metal." Spirit will become detached from "its material matrix" at a "critical point simultaneously of emergence and emersion, of maturation and escape."[9] Teilhard raises the possibility that the human consciousness which we know only as rooted in the physiological functioning of the human body may so intensify and free itself from the limitations of the body that it finally reaches a "take-off point," so to speak.

Teilhard's understanding of the relationship between matter and spirit is tied to his theology of the incarnation. Only by becoming one with the earth can Jesus fill all things. This is also our way to God; we can be saved only by becoming one with the universe. Teilhard loved the earth and delighted in nature, from the smallest atomic particle to the vast expanses of space and time. We do not find God in opposition to matter or independently of matter, but through matter. Matter enables us to enter the world, and the world to enter us. It nourishes us and links us to everything else. The food we eat is transformed into the power of thought and love. The projects with which we struggle and the people with whom we relate are part of the development of spirit in us and in them as well. In this way the energy and potentiality of the world becomes partially personalized in us. Each of us is an "in-gathering" of the earth brought to consciousness; so when we love God, we love "with every fibre of the unifying universe."[10]

Teilhard described two fundamental currents in the universe, ascent and decline. These correspond to two kinds of energy. One is subject to dissolution and decline: as structures break down, disorder increases and energy dissipates. In contrast, the other energy, which is the spiritual energy of the within of things, impels creation to a higher state of unity; it is the energy of love. This energy of love can grow and increase in our lives even as our other energy declines. Teilhard envisioned a final separation between these opposing currents of build-up and decay, a split in the universe and an escape of spirit. Dying is the way to life: "The completion of the universe is only consummated through a death, a 'night,' a reversal, an excentration, and a quasi-depersonalisation."[11] This is true on the individual level as well as the cosmic, and gives us one possible way of viewing the process of dying. Teilhard describes a transformation which involves a descent and an ascent as the path to union. The final stage of the ascent to Christ as Center of the universe occurs only with human death. In death we make a final descent into the depths of matter, but in the last great paradox of matter, death is transformed into life.

## The Anointing of the Sick: Sign of Hope in a Community of Love

The diminishments that occur during the last stages of life harm the human spirit as well as the human body. We can find no meaning in them. Why should a brilliant, witty mind be dimmed? Why must I bear the paralyzing effects of a stroke that make it impossible for me to do things for myself and put such a strain on my care-givers? Why should I be losing my memory, or my ability to see, hear, or walk? Do these things have any purpose? Where will I find the courage to bear them? Along with these unanswerable questions, the serious and chronic illnesses of the later years often lead to depression and the depletion of my emotional resources. They can make me self-centered or strain my relationships with those I love. They affect my life of faith as well. Older people experiencing the slow deterioration of disease often find themselves angry with God, or they feel distant from a God who seems to have forgotten them. Relating to God becomes as difficult as relating to friends and family.

The sacrament of anointing is directed to just such questions and experiences. In the past, we may have thought of it as a last minute ceremony performed on a Christian at the point of death. The name generally used for the sacrament, "extreme unction," reinforced this notion. Today we are recapturing its original meaning as a ritual which brings the power of Christ and the strength and comfort of the Christian community to persons facing the mystery of sickness and human fragmentation, even when death itself is not an immediate prospect.[12] Anointing touches several dimensions of the process of diminishment we have called dying.

Sickness often separates a person from the human community. The rite of anointing is intended to bring the support of the Christian community to the person experiencing illness or old age. In this way it affirms that the person is not alone in his or her suffering. The liturgical action of the laying on of hands is a physical symbol of this personal presence of the community. Through human touch the sick person is called from isolation into community. Although the sacrament may have been given very individualistically in the past, today at least some of the Christian community to which the individual belongs should be a part of the ceremony. Even when others cannot be present, the minister represents the community. When baptized, the person now being anointed was initiated into the Christian community; as he or she enters into the final and often most critical phase of that initiation into Christ, the community visibly fulfills the pledge of support they made in the baptismal liturgy. This pledge of support is broader than the anointing ritual itself. It includes all the ways in which the Christian community comes to the sick person's assistance: visiting, providing practical help with physical needs, praying with him or her, or reading and reflecting on the Scriptures together.

The sacrament of anointing also addresses the question of meaninglessness. Often the attitude of those facing illness and the diminishments of aging is one of quiet resignation. "You just have to endure." "I have to put up with it; what else can you do?" There is no ultimate answer to the mystery of human suffering. But the ritual of anointing leads the sick person to see his or her suffering as a participation in the paschal mystery of Christ's death and resurrection. Instead of being separated from God because of the illness, the person can move closer to God. Participation in the sacrament is an act of faith. At precisely that point when it is most difficult to believe and hope, the person experiences with others in the Christian community that the death and resurrection of Jesus is in fact the key to human existence. Anointing enacts in symbol Paul's words on dying and rising with Christ which we explored above.

Physical healing may result from the sacrament of anointing, but that is not its primary purpose. It is to strengthen and heal the entire person, since sickness affects our whole personality.

> If the sick person finds himself at the end of his passage ... reintegrated with himself as human person, with his community and his God, transformed by a confrontation with mortality which has been opened out into a future enriched and extended, surely he has been healed, for the humanity which was disrupted has, in the most profound sense, been made whole, whatever the physical condition of the body.[13]

Because the sacrament of anointing aims at a recovery of hope, it brings the grace to overcome anxiety and despair.

These reflections on the meaning of the paschal mystery of Christ found in Paul, Teilhard de Chardin, and the sacrament of anointing provide the context in which a Christian faces the next question we will consider—a person's right to die.

## The Right To Die

One final dimension of the theology of dying is the ethical issue of the right to die. Now that the dying process can be expanded by artificially sustaining certain vital functions, the question arises: How long should this process be drawn out? May life be shortened? Many complex issues surround actions which directly or indirectly hasten death, especially in the case of a terminal illness where a person faces a future of unrelieved pain or unconscious existence. Controversy continues to mark discussion of these issues.

Part of the discussion centers on the question of euthanasia, a term which is Greek for a "good death." Ethicists refer to two kinds of euthanasia: (1) positive, active, or direct euthanasia, and (2) negative, passive, or indirect euthanasia. Direct euthanasia (or mercy killing, as it is sometimes called) involves positive intervention which brings about death, such as an injection or an overdose of sleeping pills or other medication. The consensus against it is still strong both among most ethicists and within the medical profession. The circumstances of the elderly in our culture contribute to this caution. We live in a society that devalues the aging and fails to find use for their lives. In addition, abuse of the elderly may be on the rise.

Indirect or passive euthanasia concerns our right to die. It has become a more pressing concern now that advances in medicine mean that persons with previously fatal illnesses can be maintained at minimal functioning even though they are unable to experience life in any meaningful way. Speaking to a group of anesthesiologists on November 24, 1957, Pope Pius XII emphasized a person's right to die in dignity. There is no obligation, he said, to use extraordinary means to preserve life. We are not obliged to apply useless therapy which simply extends the dying process when there is no hope of recovery. In both Church and society there is now wide acceptance of this principle that we may withhold life supports from certain patients who suffer incurable diseases, are unconscious, or experience hopeless pain.

So that patients can make well-informed decisions about whether or not to refuse treatment, they have a right to know the truth about their illness. The Patient's Bill of Rights, approved by the American Hospital Association's House of Delegates on February 6, 1973, contains one formulation of this right. It states that patients have a right to obtain from their physicians complete information about their diagnosis, treatment, and prognosis, in terms they can reasonably be expected to understand. If it is not medically advisable to give this information to a patient, it should be made available to an appropriate person on his or her behalf. In addition to such statements of a patient's rights, many states have passed Natural Death Acts which provide a patient with the right to refuse treatment. Many of these apply only after a patient has been informed that he or she has a terminal illness, however, and therefore do not cover cases where a patient cannot be informed of the illness because of mental incompetence or unconsciousness.

Recognizing the fact that we may not always be able to express our will in this regard when we arrive at a hospital, many elderly persons are now signing living wills, directing their physicians to withhold life supports under appropriate circumstances. While these documents are not legally binding, they can be signed when one is still competent to do so, and can help physicians decide whether to initiate or continue life supports when patients are no longer able to express their wishes in the matter. Living wills can usually be obtained from law offices or senior centers, and are generally filed with one's regular physician.

We have explored several areas that can contribute to a Christian understanding of the process of dying: St. Paul's writings on the loss of our old self and the birth of a new one, Teilhard de Chardin's reflections on diminishment and the spiritualization of matter, and the strengthening of the sick and dying that comes through the sacrament of anointing. Such considerations are incomplete, however, without a longer look at the other side of dying, the Christian belief in life after death. We turn to that topic in our final chapter.

# *10*

# **RESURRECTION**

Toward the end of her life, Katharine S. White, the fiction editor of *The New Yorker,* retired to Maine with her husband, the essayist E. B. White. There she grew flowers, planning and supervising the planting of bulbs in her garden each fall until the last. In his introduction to her posthumous book, *Onward and Upward in the Garden,* her husband writes:

> As the years went by and age overtook her, there was something comical yet touching in her bedraggled appearance on this awesome occasion—the small, hunched-over figure, her studied absorption in the implausible notion that there would be yet another spring, oblivious to the ending of her own days, which she knew perfectly well was near at hand, sitting there with her detailed chart under those dark skies in the dying October, calmly plotting the resurrection.[1]

The resurrection is the implausible notion that sustains us as Christians; the deepest grace of winter is the faith that there will be yet another spring. Resurrection is one of the Christian beliefs which seems to be more important to older people than to young. Not many young people are yet aware enough of their own mortality to spend much time thinking about the meaning of an afterlife. Death, if it comes to them, enters as an intruder, robbing them of their normal life span. But when death comes at the end of a long life, its slow approach prompts reflection on the meaning of life after death.

Although the resurrection remains a mystery we cannot completely fathom, it is an essential theme of prayer and meditation in later life. Especially when we are face to face with the forces of diminishment, we need to contemplate the other side of dying. This chapter seeks to nourish such contemplation by exploring four key elements of resurrection faith: (1) the God revealed in the resurrection, (2) the resurrection as transformation, (3) resurrection and community, and (4) resurrection as a present reality.

## The God Revealed in the Resurrection

As we face the last decades of our lives, we may find ourselves asking the question of the future from fear rather than from hope. Our relationship with God changes as our life experiences change, and we may wrestle with doubts about a God who could allow the loss and suffering that the later years often bring. Even when suffering has not touched our lives personally, we have seen its power in the world over the course of many generations. We ask again the question of earlier years, perhaps now with greater urgency: "Who is this God in whom we believe?"

The God who raises Jesus is clearly a God of surprises, a God who continually creates new and unexpected things. The resurrection reveals a God who brings good out of suffering and failure, a God who calls forth life from death. With the raising of Jesus, not all has yet been done. The end of death's dominion still lies in the future, when God's

Kingdom will be revealed in its fullness. But the resurrection shows us that God is faithful to the divine promises. The message of the resurrection is that God is able to bring wholeness and integration from the disintegration and diminishment of death. Belief in the resurrection does not explain the presence of evil in the world, nor enable us to move through it easily. But the mystery of the cross and resurrection of Jesus does reveal that evil does not have the final word, good does; death is not ultimate, the God of life is.

Only living communion with such a God can sustain faith in life after death. The opening up of a new sphere of life after death is a special gift of God.[2] Jesus' resurrection confirms the fact that even death cannot destroy communion with the living God; not even suffering and death can separate us from God. The theologian Daniel O'Hanlon expresses his personal belief in this presence of God experienced now in life and continuing in some form after death.

> I do not think so much of afterlife as a time. I think of the reality of God as a present reality and as an abiding reality and of my connection with that as something that is basic and will remain. I think of reality not as a place but as a way of being. I do not have particular images of it. . . . There is the sense of that deep part of my being which is in touch with the deep reality of the divine, and there is no reason why that should cease to be just because my body wears out.[3]

This connection between communion with God and survival after death is often expressed by saying that we can entrust ourselves to God in death, or that the person who is faithful to God is somehow in the hands of God.

## The Resurrection as Transformation

In one section of Nikos Kazantzakis' novel *The Greek Passion,* the young idealist, Michelis, is agonizing with his friends over the pain, sickness, sin, and suffering in the world. Michelis cries out, "How can God let us live on the earth?" Priest Fotis responds to Michelis' question with the image of the caterpillar. It is hidden in winter within a tightly shut shroud, but one spring morning it will emerge as a butterfly. In the same way, priest Fotis concludes, deliverance is slowly and ceaselessly at work in us through the darkness. As the group ponders his words, a white orange-spotted butterfly flutters for an instant above their five heads. Then it flies off, climbs very high, and is lost in the sun.[4]

The butterfly is an ancient symbol of Christian resurrection because it embodies the notion of transformation or metamorphosis. The biblical narratives try to convey this same truth as they describe the disciples' Easter experience of the risen Jesus. Christians are promised that their own resurrection will be patterned on that of Jesus. Our interest in these narratives is therefore not only what they tell us about Jesus' resurrection, but also what they suggest about our own.

While the resurrection narratives differ in detail, they all stress that it is Jesus himself who is seen, but a Jesus who has been radically changed. The risen Jesus is different and difficult to recognize.

Now as they talked this over, Jesus himself came up and walked by their side; but something prevented them from recognizing him (Lk 24:16).

> As she (Mary of Magdala) said this she turned
> round and saw Jesus standing there, though she
> did not recognize him (Jn 20:15).

The resurrection of Jesus breaks out of our ordinary cate-
gories of time and space; theologians call it an eschatologi-
cal event, which means that in it the final age has already
begun. It is hard for the Gospel writers to find words to
describe it. Their accounts tell us that Jesus is not restored
to his former bodily life; in other words, he is not resusci-
tated the way Lazarus, Jairus' daughter, or the son of the
widow of Naim was. Rather, Jesus has been raised to a
whole new mode of existence. There is continuity but
change, identity but difference, between the earthly Jesus
the disciples knew and the risen Jesus who now appears to
them. The experience they have of Jesus' presence after his
death is no longer limited to one space; he is no longer
bound by the patterns of contact and communication
which characterize ordinary life; he suddenly appears and
then disappears. They experience in Jesus a breakthrough
into great freedom, a breakthrough which Jesus promises
they will also know in their own deaths. Resurrection, for
Jesus and his followers, is an experience of transformation.

In response to questions that the Christians in Corinth
have about the resurrection, Paul suggests some analogies
for the bodily transformation it involves. He uses the image
of a kernel of grain sown in the ground only to emerge as
wheat. If we were planting a seed for the first time, we could
not begin to imagine the wonderful full-grown plant that
comes from it as it dies in the dark soil. So it is, Paul says,
with the resurrection of the dead.

> What is sown is perishable; what is raised is
>     imperishable. It is sown in dishonor; it is raised

>in glory. It is sown in weakness; it is raised in power. It is sown a physical body; it is raised a spiritual body (1 Cor 15:35ff).

From Paul's comments to the Corinthians it is clear that he believes in a bodily resurrection. But it is a glorified body, one which belongs to the age to come. When Paul speaks of a physical and spiritual body here he is contrasting our present natural body with a Spirit-filled existence, like that of Jesus who became "a life-giving spirit" (1 Cor 15:45).

The Gospel writers emphasize that the earthly Jesus is one with the risen Jesus. This element of identity or continuity in resurrection has many important implications for the way we see our lives. The biblical scholar Raymond Brown sums up this significance very clearly. He says that in understanding God's ultimate purpose in creating, we usually think in terms of two models, either that of destruction and creation anew, or that of transformation of the existing creation.

>Will the material world pass away and all be made anew, or will somehow the world be transformed and changed into the city of God? The model that the Christian chooses will have an effect on his or her attitude toward the world and toward the corporeal. What will be destroyed can have only a passing value; what is to be transformed retains its importance. Is the body a shell that one sheds, or is it an intrinsic part of the personality that will forever identify a person?[5]

Brown holds that the resurrection of Jesus was a bodily one, and the model of transformation is therefore the one that should govern our thinking. The future is linked to the present. God will redeem our fallen world, and that includes our material world. Efforts to work for justice and peace in the world are essential aspects of belief in the resurrection. Though we cannot create a perfect world, our struggle to remove hunger, prejudice, violence, and war from the world prepares the way for God's final coming, when these efforts will be preserved and brought to fulfillment.

## Resurrection and Community

Faith in bodily resurrection is belief in the survival and transformation of our entire personhood and in the preservation of all that is really valuable to us. To understand what this means, it is important to recall the biblical understanding of the body. The biblical writers never held to a dichotomy between body and soul. They saw the person as a unity, as a body enlivened by spirit, and all of the person, body and soul, as longing for God.[6]

Although the Bible does not distinguish between body and soul, it does distinguish between flesh and spirit. These two sets of terms are by no means synonymous. Flesh refers not to the body, but to human weakness and vulnerability, to our human perishability and powerlessness. The opposite of flesh is spirit, and spirit is the power and creativity of God. It is life and vitality. When the biblical writers speak of flesh or spirit, they are referring to the whole way a person exists, as separated from God and under the power of sin, or as animated by God's power and love. Faith in the resurrection is faith in the possibility of our body, our total existence, becoming Spirit-filled, filled with the creativity of God and with God's life. Such a spiritual body, as Paul calls it, will no longer be subject to the flesh, that is, to the powers of sin and weakness.

There is another important aspect of the biblical understanding of the body. The Hebrew way of thinking, which comes to us in the Bible, did not regard the body as that which limits and separates us from everything else. Rather they thought the exact opposite; the body is the principle of communion with all else. It is our way of relating to other persons, and to all of creation. The body enables us to communicate with others; it is our means of seeing others and being seen by them, touching and being touched. A bodily resurrection therefore means the transformation of our relationship and communication with all others and all of creation. We long for this kind of transformation, since we are aware how fragmented and difficult such relating and communicating can be.

Through Jesus' bodily resurrection his relationship has been extended to all of creation. He is more deeply and universally present to his disciples. Since resurrection faith means that what happened to Jesus will also happen to us, we hope for the survival of the total person. And this includes a communion with all persons which is deeper and more extensive than we have known. Resurrection is not simply a search for our own limited identity; it is complete reconciliation with others. The Gospel descriptions of the Kingdom as a universal banquet, or as a reign of healing and forgiveness, show that this resurrection of the body is to extend to all of this world and all humankind.

Sometimes interest in the question of an afterlife becomes simply a preoccupation with the continuation of my own individual existence. That is not the Christian perspective. The New Testament makes clear that resurrection is a community experience; in fact, it involves the entire creation. What happened in Jesus' resurrection concerns nothing less than the meaning and destiny of the whole world. It implies a mission of justice, peace and love. Bodily resurrection affirms the lasting importance of the social dimensions of our lives. What will be transformed in resurrection is all of our relationships and bonds of communion. This question of relationships is, after all, one of our deepest questions about death. We fear the loss in death of the presence of others to us and our presence to them.

This understanding of bodily resurrection is actually in keeping with the sense many older people have that they live on in their gifts to others. The violinist, Alexander Schneider, who was much affected by the death of the Spanish cellist and composer, Pablo Casals, says it this way: "When a friend dies, whatever he gave you, try to augment it in thousands and thousands of ways, and give it to others—that's the only possible way."[7] Bodily resurrection, when correctly understood, involves something of this kind of lack of self-centeredness and selfishness. It also contains something of the concern for the future conveyed by the scientist and Pulitzer Prize-winning author, Rene Jules Dubos. In an interview when he was eighty he said that every spring his most enjoyable activity was to plant trees at his Hudson Highlands place in New York, even though he knew he might not live long enough to see them grow tall and beautiful.

### Resurrection as a Present Reality

The power of the resurrection is not reserved to some future age; it is now at work in our lives. Like St. Paul, John in his Gospel images the central Christian mystery in terms of a grain of wheat which dies to produce an abundant harvest. But he declares that this future fullness is also a present reality: "I tell you most solemnly, the hour will come—in fact it is here already—when the dead will hear the voice of the Son of God, and all who hear it will live" (5:25). The

Christian disciple decides here and now for life or death, and Christian love is the sign that we have passed from death to life (1 Jn 3:14). John's entire Gospel stresses the fact that we already experience the resurrection gift of the Spirit; the new age is with us now. For this reason, our own Christian experience is one source we can turn to for an understanding of resurrection from the dead.[8]

What does this mean? That those realities which destroy and separate are now weaker than what heals and unites. Every healing is thus a partial resurrection. William Johnston, in *Silent Music,* explains this relationship between healing and resurrection. He says that it can best be understood by looking at the wounds of the risen Christ. Though the wounds are still there and are not removed by the resurrection, they are now transfigured. This same kind of resurrection occurs when the hurts of our lives are healed through the experience of love.[9] A seventy-three year old man describes his sense of the relationship between life here and life after death.

> Of course, I may panic when Death knocks on my door, but as of now I see Death as introducing me to a new adventure. Life in my present state of existence has always been an adventure—loving, seeking, finding fulfillment in part and then finding new goals to beckon me on. After the death of my body, the excitement will surely not be gone; it may increase. I take with me into my new existence all that I have become, and I will perhaps find a freer chance to become even more.[10]

The psychologist Carl Jung shows us that this pattern of death and new life can be found in the experience of human growth. He describes the stages on the way to individuation or personal maturity as experiences of death and rebirth: the child leaves the womb, the adolescent enters adult life, the adult moves through the crises of middle age to true selfhood, the person leaves this world in death. Life comes through death, not apart from it. And some of us are never fully born because we fear the loss that accompanies each of these stages of growth.

We glimpse the resurrection only in poetry and paradox. In *A Grief Observed,* his reflections on the loss of his wife, C. S. Lewis muses on the reality of heaven, and refers to "that impression which I can't describe except by saying that it's like the sound of a chuckle in the darkness. The sense that some shattering and disarming simplicity is the real answer."[11] An older man I know, whose body is very bent and painful from several chronic diseases, says that the closest he can come to a glimpse of resurrection is through a recurring dream he has had during these last years. In the dream he swims all the way to a new city, and when he steps from the water, his skin is once again smooth, clear and healthy.

We saw earlier that the Spirit is the Easter gift of Jesus and is already transforming our existence in anticipation of a total transformation at the end of time. The Spirit has long been seen as the source of Christian freedom and love. Each of these realities suggests something of the experience of risen life.[12] Many older people report that with aging they experience an increase of freedom. They are less dependent on human opinion, more willing to take risks and to stand up for what they believe. Some are finally able to move beyond fears that have bound them for much of their lives. As one woman said, "It can be a pleasure to strip down to the essentials. During my middle age I overextended myself. Now I have a new freedom to pull back, to let go of some of the activities and things that cluttered my life. I've come to see that we really do enter the Kingdom only through a narrow gate, and I cherish this growing simplicity in my life." An eighty year old man discovered that for the first time he was able to be free of his negativities and to look at life with joy. "Where the Spirit of the Lord is, there is freedom," says Paul (2 Cor 3:17). The New Testament also speaks of the Spirit as the gift of love. Genuine love gives us a glimpse of resurrection. It promises to be forever. As Augustine said, "Give me a lover and he will understand the resurrection." Love reaches beyond the limits imposed by time and death and suggests something of God's love revealed in the resurrection.

We can also understand this aspect of the resurrection by listening to what Jesus said about the Kingdom of God. His images of the Kingdom are very concrete, and he makes clear that the Kingdom begins now. In fact, we are responsible for helping to bring it about. The fullness of the future is related to our present actions. This belief sustains an active love up to the end of our lives. An eighty-seven year old man with whom I worked told me, as he was recovering from a stroke, that the only reason he feared death was that it might prevent his finishing a song he was working on called "Ban the Bomb." He was writing the song because he hoped that it might save some of the children of the world from nuclear death, and he was preoccupied with the desire to complete it before his own death.

The elderly know that our lives are a series of births and deaths. They know that resurrection is always a miracle of the gift of new life, however it may come. They are ready, then, to see death as a prelude to yet another birth. As Gerard Manley Hopkins says in his poem, "The Wreck of the Deutschland," they are ready to:

Let him easter in us, be a dayspring to the
dimness of us, be a crimson-cresseted east.[13]

Resurrection is always preceded by powerlessness; it is
always the miracle of being given new life.

Not only do older people find in their present experiences of dying and rising reasons to hope in the reality of
life after death. They offer that hope to us all. For in the
paradoxes of their lives—strength in the midst of frailty,
perseverance in the midst of brokenness, love despite pain
and suffering, spiritual ascent transcending physical
decline, faith and life-engagement at the edge of death—
they witness to that miracle of new life which is the heart
of the Christian faith. Older persons are winter grace not
just for themselves and for each other, but for all of us.

# NOTES

## 1. Spirituality and Aging

1. (New York: Simon and Schuster, 1980).
2. *The Old Ones of New Mexico* (Albuquerque: University of New Mexico Press, 1973), p. 4.
3. *May Sarton. Collected Poems 1930–1973* (New York: W. W. Norton and Company, 1974), pp. 409–410.
4. (New York: Harper and Row, 1974), p. 39.
5. See James A. Peterson and Barbara Payne, *Love in the Later Years. The Emotional, Physical, Sexual and Social Potential of the Elderly* (New York: Association Press, 1975), p. 145.
6. *The Prophetic Imagination* (Philadelphia: Fortress Press, 1978).
7. (New York: Holt, Rinehart and Winston, 1979), pp. 336–338.
8. (Boston: Little, Brown and Company, 1972), pp. 196–197.
9. *Last Poems,* ed. Richard Aldington (London: Martin Secker, 1933), p. 72.

## 2. A Heart of Wisdom

1. There is a fine description of this qualitative sense of time in Geri Berg and Sally Gadow, "Toward More Human Meanings of Aging: Ideals and Images From Philosophy and Art," in *Aging and the Elderly. Humanistic Perspectives in Geron-*

160

*tology,* ed. Stuart F. Spicker, *et al.* (New Jersey: Humanities Press, Inc., 1978), pp. 83–92.

2. (New York: Simon and Schuster, 1980), p. 231.

3. See Robert N. Butler, *Why Survive? Being Old in America* (New York: Harper and Row, 1975), p. 410.

4. *The Human Season. Selected Poems 1926–1972* (Boston: Houghton Mifflin Company, 1972), p. 129.

5. *The Old Ones of New Mexico* (Albuquerque: University of New Mexico Press, 1973), p. 6.

6. Samuel H. Dresner, "Remembering Abraham Heschel," *America* 146 (May 29, 1982), 414.

7. Louis Lowy, *Social Work with the Aging. The Challenge and Promise of the Later Years* (New York: Harper and Row, 1979), pp. 166–167.

8. Practical approaches to such prayer are described in Patricia Dunn and Daniel A. Helminiak, "Spiritual Practices for the Elderly," *Spirituality Today* (June 1981), 122–136.

9. *Contemplative Prayer* (New York: Doubleday and Company, 1971), p. 30. Also helpful is John Main, *Word into Silence* (New York: Paulist Press, 1981).

10. (Nashville: Abingdon Press, 1983), p. 30.

11. "On Turning Seventy," *America* 106 (November 18, 1961), 242.

12. (New York: Doubleday and Company, 1979), pp. 35–41.

## 3. Memories

1. *The Measure of My Days* (New York: Penguin Books, 1979), p. 42.

2. "The Life Review: An Interpretation of Reminiscence in the Aged," *Psychiatry* 26 (1963), pp. 65–76. For other helpful reflections see William M. Clements, *Care and Counseling of the Aging* (Philadelphia: Fortress Press, 1979), pp. 45–62, and *The Uses of Reminiscence. New Ways of Working with Older Adults,* ed. Marc Kaminsky (New York: The Haworth Press, 1984).

3. *Early Christian Rhetoric. The Language of the Gospel* (rev. ed.; Cambridge: Harvard University Press, 1971), p. 67.
4. *Tell Me a Riddle* (New York: Dell Publishing Company, 1961), pp. 1–2.
5. (San Francisco: Harper & Row, 1982), pp. 20–21.
6. *The Hebrew Scriptures* (New York: Oxford University Press, 1978), p, 368.
7. *Messengers of God. Biblical Portraits and Legends,* trans. Marion Wiesel (New York: Random House, 1976), p. 149.
8. *America* 106 (November 18, 1961), pp. 242–245.
9. *Journal of a Soul,* trans. Dorothy White (New York: McGraw-Hill Book Company, 1965), pp. 342–343.
10. See, for example, *Healing Life's Hurts* (New York: Paulist Press, 1978), and *Healing of Memories* (New York: Paulist Press, 1974).
11. (St. Louis: The Institute of Jesuit Sources, 1978), p. 68.
12. *Gerard Manley Hopkins. Poems and Prose,* ed. W. H. Gardner (Baltimore: Penguin Books, 1953), p. 63.
13. *Identity: Youth and Crisis* (New York: W. W. Norton, 1968), pp. 139–140.
14. (New York: Simon and Schuster, 1978), p. 256.

## 4. Dependence and Independence

1. Margaret Clark and Barbara Anderson, *Culture and Aging* (Springfield, Illinois: Charles C. Thomas, 1967), p. 222.
2. "The Pollution of Time," *The Center Magazine* 4 (September–October 1971), 9.
3. *Morning Worship and Other Poems* (New York: Harcourt, Brace and Company, 1960), p. 15.
4. *The Story of Helen Keller and Anne Sullivan Macy* (New York: Delacorte Press, 1980).
5. *Widowhood in the American City* (Cambridge: Schenkman Publishing Company, 1973).
6. (New Jersey: Prentice-Hall, 1973).

7. Howard Webber, "Games," *The New Yorker* (March 30, 1963), 43.
8. Also helpful on this topic are Victoria E. Bumagin and Catherine E. Hirn, *Aging Is a Family Affair* (New York: Thomas Y. Crowell, 1979), and Barbara Silverstone and Helen Kandel Hyman, *You and Your Aging Parents* (New York: Pantheon Books, 1976).
9. Margaret Blenkner, "Social Work and Family Relationships in Later Life," in *Social Structure and the Family: Generational Relations,* ed. Ethel Shanas and Gordon F. Streib (New Jersey: Prentice-Hall, 1965), pp. 1–13.

## 5. *Love and Sexuality*

1. "The Old Gray Couple," in *New and Collected Poems 1917–1976* (Boston: Houghton Mifflin, 1976), p. 35.
2. *Selected Poems of Edwin Arlington Robinson* (New York: The Macmillan Company, 1965), pp. 24–25.
3. *Second Thoughts. Reflections on Literature and on Life* (Cleveland: The World Publishing Company, 1961), p. 151.
4. See, for example, Barbara Gallatin Anderson, *The Aging Game: Success, Sanity, and Sex After 60* (New York: McGraw-Hill, 1980); Robert N. Butler and Myrna I. Lewis, *Love and Sex After Sixty: A Guide for Men and Women in Their Later Years* (New York: Harper and Row, 1977); R. L. Solnick (ed.), *Sexuality and Aging* (Los Angeles: University of California Press, 1978).
5. P. 143.
6. Babette Deutsch, "Stranger Than the Worst," in *The Collected Poems* (New York: Doubleday and Company, 1969), p. 3.
7. (New York: Dell Publishing Company, 1961), p. 63.
8. Marjorie Lowenthal and Clayton Haven, "Interaction and Adaptation: Intimacy as a Critical Variable," in *Middle Age and Aging. A Reader in Social Psychology,* ed. Bernice L.

Neugarten (Chicago: University of Chicago Press, 1968), pp. 390–400.

9. Butler and Lewis, *Love and Sex after Sixty,* p. 137.

10. "Interaction and Adaptation," p. 400.

11. Bernard Cooke explores these aspects of friendship in *Sacraments and Sacramentality* (Connecticut: Twenty-Third Publications, 1983), pp. 83–93.

12. In Don Gold, *Until the Singing Stops* (New York: Holt, Rinehart and Winston, 1979), pp. 49–50.

13. James B. Nelson develops this dimension of sexuality in *Embodiment: An Approach to Sexuality and Christian Theology* (Minneapolis: Augsburg Publishing Company, 1978).

14. *Collected Poems 1930–1976* (New York: Oxford University Press, 1976), p. 322.

15. *Mrs. Stevens Hears the Mermaids Singing* (New York: W. W. Norton and Company, 1975), p. 211.

16. (Nashville: Abingdon Press, 1983), pp. 172–176.

17. William D. Miller, *A Harsh and Dreadful Love. Dorothy Day and the Catholic Worker Movement* (New York: Liveright, 1973), p. 349.

## 6. Older Women

1. Blanch Williams, "A Profile of the Elderly Woman," in *The Older Woman. Lavender Rose or Gray Panther,* ed. Marie Fuller and Cora Martin (Springfield, Illinois: Charles C. Thomas, 1980), pp. 5–8.

2. Elisa Melamed, *Mirror, Mirror. The Terror of Not Being Young* (New York: Simon and Schuster, 1983), p. 23.

3. "The Double Standard of Aging," *Saturday Review of Society,* 95 (September 23, 1972), pp. 29–38.

4. In Don Gold, *Until the Singing Stops* (New York: Holt, Rinehart and Winston, 1979), p. 256.

5. (New York: Crossroad Publishing Company, 1981), p. 36.

6. *The Women Around Jesus,* p. 38.

7. (New York: G. P. Putnam's Sons, 1973), pp. 149–150.

8. "Spiritual Well-Being as a Celebration of Wholeness," in *Spiritual Well-Being of the Elderly,* ed. James A. Thorson and Thomas C. Cook, Jr. (Springfield, Illinois: Charles C. Thomas, 1980), p. 204.
9. This theme is developed by Carol Gilligan, *In a Different Voice* (Cambridge: Harvard University Press, 1982).
10. *Collected Poems 1930–1973* (New York: W. W. Norton and Company, 1974), p. 76.
11. *Receiving Woman. Studies in the Psychology and Theology of the Feminine* (Philadelphia: Westminster Press, 1981), p. 21.

## 7. Humor and Hope

1. *Messengers of God. Biblical Portraits and Legends,* trans. Marion Wiesel (New York: Random House, 1976), p. 86.
2. (New York: The Bobbs-Merrill Company, 1969), p. 357.
3. *The Transcendent Self. Formative Spirituality of the Middle, Early, and Later Years of Life* (New Jersey: Dimension Books, 1979), p. 12.
4. *Lunacy and Letters,* ed. Dorothy Collins (New York: Sheed and Ward, 1958), p. 97.
5. Peter Berger develops this idea in *A Rumor of Angels. Modern Society and the Rediscovery of the Supernatural* (New York: Doubleday and Company, 1970), pp. 69–72.
6. *Homo Viator. Introduction to a Metaphysic of Hope* (New York: Harper and Row, 1965), pp. 49–50.
7. (New York: The New American Library, 1966).
8. *Eclipse of God: Studies in the Relation Between Religion and Philosophy,* trans. Maurice Friedman (New York: Harper and Row, 1957), p. 6.
9. *The Desert Blooms* (Nashville: Abingdon Press, 1983), pp. 188–189.
10. In Eugene Bianchi, *Aging as a Spiritual Journey* (New York: Crossroad Publishing Company, 1982), p. 238.

11. *Homo Viator,* p. 62.
12. (New York: Harper and Row, 1967), p. 21.


### 8. Loss


1. Robert N. Butler, *Why Survive? Being Old in America* (New York: Harper and Row, 1975), p. 174.
2. (Boston: Houghton Mifflin Company, 1982), p. 20.
3. *Modern Man in Search of a Soul* (New York: Harcourt, Brace and World, 1933), p. 109.
4. See, for example, several of the studies in *Middle Age and Aging. A Reader in Social Psychology,* ed. Bernice L. Neugarten (Chicago: University of Chicago Press, 1968).
5. (New York: Random House, 1974).
6. *Process and Reality* (New York: Macmillan Company, 1929), p. 400.
7. Robert Hirschfield, "My Mother Teaches Me What It's Like To Be Old in America," *The National Catholic Reporter* (June 19, 1981), p. 13.
8. (New York: Seabury Press, 1979), p. 71. See also Nancy L. Mace and Peter V. Rabins, *The Thirty-Six Hour Day: A Family Guide to Caring for Persons with Alzheimer's Disease* (Baltimore: Johns Hopkins University Press, 1981).
9. *Process and Reality,* pp. 407–408. Helpful explanations of this aspect of Whitehead's thought are found in William A. Beardslee, *A House for Hope* (Philadelphia: Westminster Press, 1972), and Marjorie Hewitt Suchocki, *God, Christ, Church. A Practical Guide to Process Theology* (New York: Crossroad Publishing Company, 1982).
10. *The Divine Milieu* (New York: Harper and Row, 1960), pp. 55–56.
11. *Process and Reality,* p. 408.
12. *Gerard Manley Hopkins. Poems and Prose,* ed. W. H. Gardner (Baltimore: Penguin Books, 1953), p. 54.

## 9. Dying

1. "The Love Song of J. Alfred Prufrock," in *The Complete Poems and Plays. 1909-1950* (New York: Harcourt Brace and World, 1952), p. 6.
2. Quoted in Robert N. Butler, *Why Survive? Being Old in America* (New York: Harper and Row, 1975), p. 79.
3. (New Mexico: Iroquois House, 1982), pp. 193–194.
4. *The Divine Milieu* (New York: Harper and Row, 1960), p. 76.
5. Ibid., p. 82.
6. *The Habit of Being,* ed. Sally Fitzgerald (New York: Random House, 1979), p. 509.
7. *The Divine Milieu,* pp. 89–90.
8. *The Measure of My Days* (New York: Penguin Books, 1979), pp. 13–14.
9. Teilhard de Chardin, *The Phenomenon of Man* (New York: Harper and Row, 1959), p. 288.
10. Ibid., p. 297.
11. *The Divine Milieu,* p. 93.
12. Helpful discussions of the sacrament of anointing are found in James L. Empereur, *Prophetic Anointing. God's Call to the Sick, the Elderly, and the Dying* (Delaware: Michael Glazier, Inc., 1982), and Joseph Martos, *Doors to the Sacred* (New York: Doubleday and Company, 1981).
13. M. Jennifer Glen, "Sickness and Symbol: The Promise of the Future," *Worship* 54 (September 1980), p. 408.

## 10. Resurrection

1. (New York: Farrar, Straus, Giroux, 1979), p. xix.
2. Edward Schillebeeckx develops this notion in *Christ. The Experience of Jesus as Lord,* trans. John Bowden (New York: Crossroad Publishing Company, 1981), pp. 797ff.
3. In Eugene C. Bianchi, *Aging as a Spiritual Journey* (New York: Crossroad Publishing Company, 1982), p. 255.

4. (New York: Simon and Schuster, 1953), pp. 168–169.
5. *The Virginal Conception and Bodily Resurrection of Jesus* (New York: Paulist Press, 1973), pp. 128–129).
6. H. J. Richards describes the meaning of bodily resurrection well in *The First Easter. What Really Happened?* (London: Fontana Books, 1976).
7. In Don Gold, *Until the Singing Stops* (New York: Holt, Rinehart and Winston, 1979), p. 189.
8. Helpful suggestions for deepening our understanding of resurrection are found in H. A. Williams, *True Resurrection* (New York: Harper and Row, 1972).
9. (New York: Harper and Row, 1974), p. 121.
10. C. G. Wrenn, "The Future of a Person—Me," *Personnel and Guidance Journal* 54 (1975), 20.
11. (New York: Seabury Press, 1961), p. 83.
12. See Gerald O'Collins, *What Are They Saying About the Resurrection?* (New York: Paulist Press, 1978).
13. *Gerard Manley Hopkins. Poems and Prose,* ed. W. H. Gardner (Baltimore: Penguin Books, 1953), p. 24.

# SUGGESTIONS FOR FURTHER READING

Bianchi, Eugene C. *Aging as a Spiritual Journey.* New York: Crossroad Publishing Company, 1982.

Blythe, Ronald. *The View in Winter: Reflections on Old Age.* New York: Harcourt Brace Jovanovich, 1979.

Clements, William M., ed. *Ministry with the Aging. Designs, Challenges, Foundations.* New York: Harper and Row, 1981.

Cook, Thomas C., Jr., ed. *The Religious Sector Explores Its Mission in Aging.* Georgia: National Interfaith Coalition on Aging, 1976.

Fisher, M. F. K. *Sister Age.* New York: Alfred A. Knopf, 1983.

Robert M. Gray and David O. Moberg. *The Church and the Older Person.* Grand Rapids: William B. Eerdmans Publishing Company, 1977.

Hiltner, Seward, ed. *Toward a Theology of Aging.* New York: Human Sciences Press, 1975.

LeFevre, Carol and Perry, eds. *Aging and the Human Spirit.* Chicago: Exploration Press, 1981.

Nouwen, Henri and Gaffney, Walter. *Aging: The Fulfill-ment of Life.* New York: Doubleday and Company, 1974.

*Religion and Aging. An Annotated Bibliography.* Compiled by Vincent Fecher. San Antonio: Trinity University Press, 1982.

Staude, John-Raphael, ed. *Wisdom and Age.* Berkeley: Ross Books, 1981.

Thorson, James and Cook, Thomas, eds. *Spiritual Well-Being of the Elderly.* Springfield, Ill.: Charles C. Thomas, 1980.

Tiso, Francis, ed. *Aging: Spiritual Perspectives.* Florida: Sunday Publications, 1982.

Tournier, Paul. *Learn to Grow Old.* New York: Harper and Row, 1972.

Whitehead, Evelyn Eaton and James D. *Christian Life Patterns.* New York: Doubleday and Company, 1979.